THE
PSYCHEDEL
SHAMAN

try to access your Wisdom Warrior and the rituals that can expand your consciousness."

STANLEY KRIPPNER, PH.D., AUTHOR OF *A CHAOTIC LIFE* AND
HEALING STATES AND COAUTHOR OF *THE VOICE OF ROLLING THUNDER*

"Tom Pinkson offers a compelling vision of how psychedelic experiences, when approached with reverence and proper guidance, can be profound catalysts for personal and collective transformation. Drawing on more than 50 years of immersion in Indigenous wisdom traditions, Pinkson provides a much-needed roadmap for working with plant medicines in a way that honors their sacred power."

TRICIA EASTMAN, AUTHOR OF *SEEDING CONSCIOUSNESS*

"Tom Pinkson weaves an insightful and profound exploration of psychedelic shamanism based on his 50 years of direct experience with Indigenous shamans. The book invites you to transform into your version of the Warrior and delves into the ethical and responsible use of psychedelics. It offers invaluable guidance on healing trauma and connecting with cosmic love.

ITZHAK BEERY, AUTHOR OF *THE GIFT OF SHAMANISM*

"There are those who talk—and those who walk the talk—who strive to follow a path of their own creation that is relevant and uplifting to all who come to share in their presence. I have great gratitude for Tom's continued generosity of spirit and wisdom as he gives us that opportunity and offers a profound enrichment of consciousness, soul, and leads us to the sources."

PHIL WOLFSON, M.D., COEDITOR OF *THE KETAMINE PAPERS*

"Tom Pinkson's knowledge flows from a heart/mind attuned to Mother Earth and the stars and with an authenticity that comes from being comfortable with his humanity. This book is a gateway to all of that."

ALAN LEVIN, AUTHOR OF
PREPARATION FOR A SACRED PSYCHEDELIC JOURNEY

THE
PSYCHEDELIC
SHAMAN

THE WISDOM WARRIOR'S
PATH TO TRANSFORMATION

Tom Soloway Pinkson, Ph.D.

Bear & Company
Rochester, Vermont

Bear & Company
One Park Street
Rochester, Vermont 05767
www.BearandCompanyBooks.com

Bear & Company is a division of Inner Traditions International

Note to the Reader: This book is intended as an informational guide and should not be a substitute for professional medical care or treatment. Neither the author nor the publisher assumes any responsibility for physical, psychological, legal, or social consequences resulting from the ingestion of psychedelic substances or their derivatives.

Cataloging-in-Publication Data for this title is available from the Library of Congress

ISBN 978-1-59143-539-6 (print)
ISBN 978-1-59143-540-2 (ebook)

Printed and bound in India at Replika Press Pvt. Ltd.

10 9 8 7 6 5 4 3 2 1

Text design by Virginia Scott Bowman and layout by Kenleigh Manseau
This book was typeset in Garamond Premier Pro with Kelvingrove and Bookmania used as display typefaces
Artwork by Roger Clay using Midjourney

To send correspondence to the author of this book, mail a first-class letter to the author c/o Inner Traditions • Bear & Company, One Park Street, Rochester, VT 05767, and we will forward the communication.

Scan the QR code and save 25% at InnerTraditions.com. Browse over 2,000 titles on spirituality, the occult, ancient mysteries, new science, holistic health, and natural medicine.

For my grandsons, Corbin, Luke, and Sebastian.

And for all of you who know things can be better.

CONTENTS

◇◇◇◇◇◇◇◇◇◇◇◇◇◇

S T E P   I I

WISE UP

◇◇◇◇◇◇◇◇◇◇◇◇◇◇

S T E P   I I I

LIVE LOVE NOW

◇◇◇◇◇◇◇◇◇◇◇◇◇◇

S T E P   I V

THE WISDOM WARRIOR PATH

FOREWORD

Rabbi Michael Ziegler, D.Min.

Fifty years ago, very few Americans had ever heard of using the Indigenous sacred practices of fasting, meditation, ayahuasca, teo-nanacatl (mushrooms), and mescaline cactus to expand consciousness. Only a handful of anthropologists had ever visited Indigenous shamans, curanderos, and medicine men and women in the places they lived and practiced. Even fewer had the patience and commitment to learn these traditions by sitting at the feet of Indigenous elders, building trust and skills over decades.

Today the landscape has shifted, large numbers of individuals are actively seeking the kinds of expanded states of awareness that have been cultivated by premodern societies for centuries. Sacred technologies such as yoga and meditation are now widely known and readily accessible. The use of sacred plant medicines and psychedelics is following a similar trajectory.

Tom Pinkson, or tomás as he is known by those who follow his work, set out on his pilgrimage when few people in the United States had ever heard of ayahuasca or psilocybin, before the internet offered immediate access to information about plant medicines, psychedelic molecules, and the ceremonial traditions of North and South American Indigenous cultures. He offers an important perspective for those interested in these ways. As a wisdom elder, tomás has conducted thousands of ceremonies in service of healing and deepening people's understanding of themselves and their relationship to our planet.

Tom is uniquely qualified to share with modern psychonauts the wisdom traditions that lie behind the secular use of psychedelics. Tom got his Ph.D. in psychology and spent decades working with at-risk youth and children who had terminal diseases. Simultaneously, he immersed himself in Indigenous religious practices, completing an arduous Huichol apprenticeship. He has served as a bridge builder, able to share in modern vernacular and Earth-based wisdom traditions. In this book, Tom shares what he learned on his pilgrimage through Indigenous curanderismo and Western psychology. Supported in these wisdom traditions, he broke new trails as a psychologist, vision quest leader, sacred medicine ceremonialist, hospice leader, and rite of passage guide.

In this book, we travel with Tom through time, bearing witness to his journey with First Nation Elders and wisdomkeepers who guided and mentored him. He introduces us to the teachings of medicine man Rolling Thunder, Huichol Mara'akame Guadalupe de la Cruz Rios, Mazatec curandera Doña Julieta, Terence McKenna, ayahuasqueros and curanderos from the Amazon jungle, and psychiatrist Dr. Jerry Jampolsky—to name just a few of the wisdomkeepers that influenced his life. In turn, tomás shares what he has learned, acting as an adept guide skilled in fasting, pilgrimage, prayer, breathwork, grief work, end-of-life care, psychedelic journeys, mindfulness practices, and integration processes.

Tomás is a generous soul. He has been in service to others for most of his life. In his current phase of life, he explores what it means for us to age fruitfully, deployed in service to family, friends, and community. He walks the path of what he calls a "Wisdom Warrior," and a seasoned psychedelic guide. Tomás is a special individual who has explored the nooks and crannies of his soul under the guidance of wise elders. He, in turn, has sat for countless others on their personal journeys, and now brings to us a thorough, elegant, and loving distillation of what he's learned.

In light of his extraordinary experiences, tomás does not present himself from the place of enlightened spirituality. His voice, in his book as in life, is one of a fellow traveler. No better. No worse. Just a fellow human swimming in the soup of life, interdependently connected with all of humanity and creation in love and compassion.

Tomás has a wry sense of humor and a disarming smile; he carries joy with him. He has been on the road long enough to have inhabited a full measure of human experience.

There is a Jewish story from the first century in which a seeker comes to the humble Rabbi Hillel and asks to be taught all of the Jewish wisdom tradition while he stands on one foot. The rabbi, undeterred, told him: "What is distasteful to you, do not do to your neighbor. That is the whole teaching of the Torah. The rest is commentary. Now—go study it."

I have been blessed to sit in ceremony with tomás, where I have observed his mastery of holding space for others who choose to traverse powerful mind states. After a ceremony, I asked tomás to teach me how he holds space as a Wisdom Warrior and psychedelic guide. In retrospect, I was requesting the whole download while I was standing on one foot. He considered my question, took a deep breath, and then thoughtfully responded:

"I try to be a clear channel for another person, to support them. Whether they are dying or in grief, on a vision quest or on a psychedelic journey, my task is to keep my heart open, noticing if anything is blocking Spirit's love flowing through me to that person; to be without attachment to changing them or making something happen.

"While I offer my presence, if something comes up in me, or between me and the person I am with, so that my heart closes through judgment or constriction—then it is my work to deal with this constriction so that my heart can reopen the pipeline and allow love's flow to come through me to that person or family, or whatever the situation.

"What happens in terms of an outcome is in bigger hands than mine. My role is to show up, with the support of my teachers and my practices, bringing the full quality of my presence to the person I am with—to support their journey and process."

The rest is commentary.

Thank you, tomás, for taking the time to share a deep well of hard-earned and love-infused wisdom. Your book is a beautiful offering we can learn from and apply to our lives and practice.

MICHAEL ZIEGLER, D.MIN., has led individuals in expanded states of consciousness for forty years. He is interested in the skillful means intersecting meditation, psychoactives, somatic practice, and meaning making—refining methods that recontextualize ancient wisdom practices for modern explorers. He curated the Guiding Presence website, which archives and open sources the wisdom of psychedelic elders. Michael was ordained by Rabbi Zalman Schachter-Shalom and has been on the faculty of Naropa University, the University of Creation Spirituality, the Chaplaincy Institute, and the California Institute of Integral Studies.

PROLOGUE

Transmission from Starlight Ohana

When we look up at the stars, we are really looking into ourselves. . . We are a way for the universe to know itself. Some part of our being knows this is where we came from. We long to return. And we can because the cosmos is also within us. We're made of star stuff.

CARL SAGAN, *COSMOS,* 1980*

I was driving north out of San Francisco, engrossed in a podcast by astrophysicist Neil deGrasse Tyson, when a statement he made struck me so profoundly I had to pull off the freeway for my own safety. What he said wasn't new information. It wasn't something I didn't already know, yet I sat there with my body electrified, as if I were a Christmas tree on steroids.

Energy streamed through my body, collapsing seventy-five years of experience to a coherent understanding of the purpose of my life and what I was to do with the remaining time I had. What had the scientist

---

*Notes in this book come from notes I saved over the years, for which I didn't write down the sources because I thought I would only be using them in my journal. As a consequence, I am not able to properly reference and honor the authors of some of these quotes. I humbly ask forgiveness from those authors and publishers for this lapse. Thank you for sharing your wisdom.

said that halted me so abruptly? I will tell you—but first, read it for yourself and see what it brings up for you: "We are stardust brought to life."

At the precise moment I heard this statement, a beam of sunlight burst through the windshield, illuminating my car with its brilliance despite the otherwise cloudy sky, and bathing me in its grandeur. Its electromagnetic photonic energy had traveled ninety-three million miles to Earth, just as it had been doing for billions of years, fueling the wheels of evolution to produce self-reflective life. In that precise moment, I realized—I was starlight come to life!

Stunned by the enormity of the evolutionary process, I thought of Paul on his way to Damascus, struck by light and transformed in his entire being. I'd been sitting in a state of amazement for an indeterminable period when a phrase began to resonate through my mind: "We are stardust brought to Earth, we are stardust brought to birth. We are stardust brought to life, to shine, shine, shine."

More phrases continued to flow. I reached for my journal on the seat beside me and started writing them down. Fourteen verses emerged, recounting the story of stardust arriving on Earth, giving birth to life through evolution, and culminating in the self-reflective consciousness that reveals our true nature, our luminosity, and our purpose in existing—to polish our stardust and radiate love into the world. It wasn't me composing—I was just hearing and transcribing the lyrics onto paper. (You'll find the full song's lyrics in the final section of this book.)

Later that day, when I got home, I put simple chords to the words and played it on my guitar. The Starlight Song told a story that summarized the teachings of the past half-century of my life. I saw how all the work I had been doing over this time—all the groups I had started, all the retreats I had led, all the vision quests, all the people I had seen and worked with in my private practice, and the WAKAN spiritual community I started in the mid-1980s—fit together in what was being revealed by this transmission from the Starlight Ohana.

Ohana is a Hawaiian word that refers to an extended family. I realized how all humanity is made of stardust, kept alive by stardust, being fed indirectly by the force of sunlight coming to plants, which are eaten in turn by animals, both of which we humans consume, thus providing us with the fuel for our lives. The song tells the story of who we are, what we are, and why we are here. It illuminates a pathway to living a meaningful life amid the challenges of today's threatened world.

I eventually recorded the song accompanied by a video, and even collaborated with my sister, artist Ilsa Pinkson-Burke, to turn it in to a children's book, *The Story of the Starlight Song*, featuring her illustrations. The message of the song encapsulates the wisdom teachings of over half a century of psychedelic shamanic visionary insights.

We are sacred, worthy, luminous beings. We are loved. We are love, and our love is for giving and receiving. We are sacred because we were made by the creative powers of the universe expressing as stardust brought to life. Because of our sacred essence, we are worthy of being respected, honored, cared for, valued, and celebrated as the miraculous, awe-inspiring, luminous manifestations of evolutionary wonder that we are.

We are not here in this life at this time by accident. We are here to Wake Up, to Wise Up, and to remember our true nature, our divinity, and our purpose—to Live the Love that we are Now.

"Open your heart and be kind. Right now is always the best time," reads one verse of the Starlight Song. Isn't that precisely what the challenges of these times we are living in call for—to be more loving and kind? To create a world based on love and cooperation, respect and caring, instead of fear and competition?

Life is an exploration of what is possible. It's a cosmic experiment to see what we humans do with the gift of life, the gift of consciousness we've been given as part of the collectivity of humanity, woven together in a web of interconnectivity and interdependence with the entire cosmos.

In 1966 I was gifted with a life-changing shamanic visionary experience, which I will describe later on in this book, and have been striving ever since to live from the love that vision showed me to be true. This goal has been a formidable challenge, given the fact that my particular nervous system's wiring makes me prone to quick judgmental reactivity, coming from an animal body with a reptilian brain and monkey mind.

It all comes down to being present in the moment, as what I call a Psychedelic Shamanic Wisdom Warrior, seeking to Wake Up, Wise Up, and Live Love Now in a universe that can be tricky to navigate. That's what I strive to do in my life, and what I try to support for fellow members of the Starlight Ohana so that, collectively, we can harness the infinite wisdom guidance available to us to successfully create a healthy, happy, just, peaceful, beautiful, rejuvenating, sustainable, Win-Win World for All.

Thus, we fulfill our purpose in being here, and thus I come to write this book and offer what I have been fortunate to learn in support of you who are reading this book right now. The more of us who skillfully work together to polish up our starlight, the sooner we can reach a critical mass of consciousness to shift our fear-based, polarized world to a love-based one that opens what the Huichol people of Mexico call the *nierica*, the cosmic portal, for the fullest blossoming and greatest good of life on Mother Earth.

THE STARLIGHT OHANA TRANSMISSION
(AKA STARLIGHT SONG)

We are all members of the Starlight Ohana
Tasked by evolution toward a new vision of living,
Polishing our stardust, shining the light of awareness
Into the divinity of our true nature.
Doing our part in unity with our sisters and brothers
to Live Love Now,
Helping to create a healthy, just, peaceful, equitable,
beautifully diverse, Win-Win World for All.
We are joining together to create spiritual community,
Feeding grids of light on Mother Earth's body with
high-frequency positive emotions.
Supporting each other,
We walk our Heart Path to Completion, using
challenges as opportunities to do the work.
We are opening cosmic doorways to bring through
the fullest blossoming
For the greatest good for All.
May it be so, and so it is!

GRATITUDES

I want to acknowledge and honor the following Indigenous medicine people with whom I have worked. Their teachings have profoundly influenced my life. The knowledge I share in this book would not be possible without their generous guidance, provided to a Caucasian man attempting to create a meaningful life. I am eternally indebted to all of my teachers and mentors, and sincerely hope I have fulfilled their request to honor their generosity by sharing the wisdom teachings of their lineage.

Great gratitude to:

Muskogee/Creek medicine man: Philip Deere
Lakota pipe holders: Good Horse Nation, J. C. Eaglesmith, Archie Fire Lame Deer, and Arvil Looking Horse
Seneca: Twylah Nitsch
Mazateca curandera: Doña Julieta
Hopi: Thomas Banyacya and Grandfather David Monongaye
Pit River/Shasta: Babe Wilson
Karuk People: Charlie Thom
Pomo-Miwok: Lanny and Irene Pinola and Bun Lucas
Hawaiian: Mits Aioki and Aunty Fay
Ayahuascaros: Anank, Bolivar, and Agustino
Mohawk: Peter Blue Cloud
Cherokee metis: Rolling Thunder
Shoshoni: Spotted Fawn

Apache metis: Bright Rope and Oh Shinnah Fastwolf
Hindu: Yogi Bhajan, Swami Satchidananda, Eknath Easwaran, A. C.
Bhaktivedanta Swami Prabhupada, and Maharishi Mahesh Yogi
Huichol: Don Jose Matsua, Guadalupe de la Cruz, Tacho, Andrea,
José Carillo, Presciliano, Ramaldo, Pedro, Maria, Laura, Jose and
Paula, Eberta, Domingo, Manuela, and Prem Das, who opened
the door through his marriage into the tribe
Native American Church: Richard Deer Track and Bob Boyll
Peruvian: Eduardo Calderon and Jim Saint Martin, art teacher at
the College of Marin and my first Indigenous mentor

I want to acknowledge and honor elders from other traditions who taught me the correct way to interact with ceremonial ways. Although I don't recall their names, I honor them by naming their People: Navajo, Mayan, Sufi, Balinese, Sammi, Druid, Buddhist, and Taoist.

I also honor a remarkable eighty-year-old grandmother from way up in the Yukon who gifted me with a magnificent pair of beaded moccasins she made herself.

In addition to the Indigenous elders, I honor the following individuals, most of whom are now in the spirit world but are not forgotten. Their teachings, support, and friendship have been instrumental in guiding me on my life path: Gary Snyder, Angeles Arrien, Stephen Gaskin, Ram Dass, Huston Smith, Leo Zeff, Terence McKenna, Robert Greenway, Edward Larry Beggs, Jerry Jampolsky, John Perry, Sasha and Ann Schulgin, Willie Unsoeld, Bill Pemberton, and Francis Vaughn.

I also appreciate the teachings of aikido instructors Richard Moon, George Leonard, Wendy Palmer and Chris Thorsen, medicine woman Camila Martinez, and philosopher George Gurdjieff. Although I didn't personally know Gurdjieff, his work on awakening has played an instrumental role in my process of Waking up, Wising up, and Living Love Now.

I honor Albert Hofmann, the father of LSD, whom I met at a weeklong gathering at the Esalen Institute, organized by Dr. Stan Grof. This gathering resembled a meeting of shamans from different Amazonian tribes, sharing their respective sacred medicines and learning from each

RALPH METZNER

other's experiences. Albert was a humble, gracious elder who encouraged me to continue my work using psychedelics in a sacred manner.

Last, I pay tribute to my close friend Ralph Metzner, a pioneer in the responsible use of psychedelics, with whom I co-led journeys and a workshop in Ireland. Ralph passed away peacefully at his home in the spring of 2019. Fortunately, I was able to visit him just prior to his passing. Although he was very weak, the power of the love-light emanating from his heart was astonishing. We celebrated our thirty-odd years of friendship with joyful gratitude.

I celebrate Ralph's life, his contributions, and our friendship by including his thoughts about love and gratitude here:

> Love is our birthright—the source from which we come. Love is about union, connection, affection, shared pleasure, and delight. Love is patient, kind, and nurturing. Love is an awareness of God's presence in each other and all creation.

Gratitude to Ralph for a life well lived. *Vaya con Dios.*

INTRODUCTION

I am the weaver. I am the woven one.
I am the dreamer. I am the dream.

LORNA KOHLER

This book is about good news. It acknowledges a creative wisdom power in the universe that is accessible at all times, ready to assist not just in survival, but also in thriving through perilous times.

This book is about becoming a Psychedelic Shamanic Wisdom Warrior for the healing of personal and planetary wounds. Living as such a Warrior means striving for authentic, soulful integrity and walking your Heart Path to Completion. It involves being an agent of conscious evolution, serving Spirit rather than ego. It means skillfully navigating your challenges to allow for the fullest blossoming and the greatest good with joy, grace, and gratitude. It's about showing up to do your part as a skillful spiritual activist, working to heal the sacred hoop of life.

Psychedelic Shamanism cultivates Wisdom Warriors. This refers to the use of time-tested shamanic practices to connect with, attune to, and commune with the underlying reality of infinite, unconditional cosmic love-light—the essence of our being—and living from that essence in, with, and through all our relations.

The term "psychedelic" derives from the Greek words *psyché*, meaning "soul, mind," and *delos*, meaning "to manifest." It translates to "mind manifesting." Respectfully used, psychedelics can open doorways

1

in the mind to an expanded awareness far beyond the narrow bandwidth of mainstream Eurocentric consciousness. This consciousness, whose materially based value system has spread globally through imperialism, settler colonialism, capitalism, and consumerism, is what we aim to transcend.

As you will discover in the following pages, the use of psychedelics has been a primary gate opener in my exploration of expanded states of awareness. Another significant gate opener has been extended solitude time spent fasting in the wilderness during vision quest experiences. The use of nature quests and mind-altering plants are ancient shamanic practices that stretch back to the Paleolithic past of our earliest human ancestors. These practices have persisted to modern times—albeit somewhat underground and certainly not with mainstream involvement, although that is changing—because of their efficacy in dissolving the boundaries of ego identity, opening the human mind to its potential for experiencing an ecstatic state of cosmic consciousness and a blissful experience of the interconnectedness of all beings and of all creation. It is a unitive state where all polarities dissolve into oneness; there is no perception of separate things or separate beings, only oneness.

The term "Psychedelic Shamanic Wisdom Warriors" refers to people who have a sense of this interconnectedness and are trying to live from the agape love that is its essence. Agape love is the highest form of love, in contrast with eros, or erotic love, and philia, or brotherly love.

There are many other ways to experience this state besides the use of psychedelics and vision questing. These include movement, listening to music, making music, singing, chanting, drumming, meditation, yoga, pranayama, praying, breathing practices, making love, T'ai Chi and Qigong practices, as well as activities that demand high levels of sustained concentration, such as rock climbing, long distance running and swimming, surfing, paddleboarding, biking, kayaking, hiking, mountaineering, and many more. All of these activities, when performed with specific intention and quality of attention, can open gateways to higher realms of awareness of the interwoven nature of reality and to our true nature, which is infinite unconditional light and love.

You don't need to use or have used psychedelics to be a Psychedelic Shamanic Wisdom Warrior. You just need to strive to live from the love that you are, knowing and trusting that you are more than your body, more than your ego, more than your stories.

Psychedelic Shamanic Wisdom Warriors do not battle with physical violence but with inner opponents that strive to close hearts and poison the mind. They bring agape love to action in the world, working for peace, justice, and equal opportunity for all. They evoke the warrior archetype but fight with the weapons of skillful communication, using the transformational energy of love to shift fear to faith, shadow to illumination, and injustice to justice. They act with love. They act from love.

Psychedelic Shamanic Wisdom Warriors strive to keep their hearts open to the flow of infinite unconditional love, which is their true nature. They live with attunement to a higher calling than ego-serving spirit—the intelligence flow of the universe—walking a love based spiritual path to transform a fear-based culture to a love-based, healthy, happy, and equitable one, to create and work for the fullest blossoming and greatest good for all people and beings of Mother Earth.

Creating a Win-Win World for All involves acknowledging the harm we as a nation have historically inflicted on Indigenous, Black, and Brown people, and the harm that continues to be wrought upon them. It requires apology and restorative justice, with reparations for that which was taken by violence. This is facing the shadow work on a national level, which is integral to transformational healing. Attempting to build a healthy society without doing so is akin to erecting a beautiful building atop a foundation of termite rot and decay. Psychedelic Shamanic Wisdom Warriors hear the call and take action.

The "how" of the action is up to the guidance in each person's heart. It is not about comparing or measuring your action as good, better, or worse than someone else's. It is not a competition with a winner or loser, because we all lose if we don't change how we, as humanity, are operating. This current way of operating has brought us to calamitous situations that threaten the future existence of our species, as well as many other species that are already dying off at an alarming rate.

To all who feel the call to Psychedelic Shamanic Wisdom Warrior ways, thank you for the courage it takes to *hana pono*, Hawaiian for "do the right thing," and for standing up for healing, for peace, for justice, and for equality for all people. Do what your heart and soul call you to do. Join a worldwide Starlight Ohana, an extended family of lightworkers supporting each other in polishing up the light we are in order to Wake Up, Wise Up, and Live Love Now, shining transformational energy to the planetary field.

As a white, heterosexual male with all the associated privileges, I have to undo the oppressive effects of colonization fueled by the ideology of white supremacy in my own mind. This belief system is deeply and subliminally embedded in the social, educational, economic, and health institutions I grew up in, and it still persists today, giving privilege to Caucasians and oppressing People of Color.

Psychedelic Shamanic Wisdom Warriors recognize that it's way past time to *pagar la manda*, to pay the debt incurred by racist, discriminatory, and unjust institutional policies motivated by greed and fed by fear that have been part of our history in this country since the very beginning. It's way past time, but better late than never, to Wake Up, Wise Up, and Live Love Now, helping to heal the Sacred Hoop.

I invite you to step in to your version of Psychedelic Shamanic Wisdom Warriorhood, working to heal your inner wounds, the wounds of humanity, and those of our Mother Earth by doing your part to create a Win-Win World for All.

May it be so for increasing numbers around the world—but remember, it always starts with you and me, here and now, this day, this sacred breath.

Love Every Step.

— tomás —

STEP ONE

Wake Up

*Bring awareness to the constrictive,
unconsciously conditioned "virtual reality software"
(thoughts, values, identity of self, nature of reality, behaviors)
that operates beneath the level of ordinary awareness,
because you cannot change what you do not see and face.*

CHAPTER 1

THE SHATTERING

We need to change the lens by which we see the world.

JEREMY LENT, *THE WEB OF MEANING*

My lens of perception and understanding was shattered two months before my fourth birthday, when my biological dad, Fred Irving Soloway, died at the young age of thirty-six. As a child, he had contracted rheumatic fever, which ravaged his heart. He fell ill again in 1937 while fighting for freedom and democracy against the fascism of Franco in the Spanish Civil War, as part of the Abraham Lincoln Brigade, and his heart never recovered. My father's death shattered the expectations about life I had learned from the stories my mother read to me at bedtime: ". . . and they all lived happily ever after."

I did not know it then, but this loss, while a shocking introduction to the teaching of impermanence, initiated a journey that eventually led me to Indigenous spirituality, psychedelics, shamanism, and quantum physics.

As a youngster, I knew my dad was sick. I had carried medicine to him in his bed more than once, careful not to spill. However, I had no idea of the severity of his condition. I never suspected or feared he would die. Instead, I felt loved, safe, and cared for. Then suddenly, he was gone, taken away.

And so was my mother. No one told me where she was. Months later, I learned that just after my dad had died, my mother had entered the hospital for emergency thyroid surgery and was hospitalized for six weeks.

During that time, I was left adrift. My baby sister Ilsa and I were shuttled around New York City, moving from one of our seven aunties to another.

"Your father's gone on a long ocean voyage," an uncle told me.

But I knew this wasn't true. I knew somehow that my dad had died and would not be coming back. I remember feeling clearly yet another loss—loss of my trust in adults for telling me the truth. I felt totally alone. *I am in this by myself,* I thought. Shell-shocked and frightened, with no one to turn to, I shut down.

I had no closure or support in dealing with my father's death because I never got to attend a funeral or memorial service, or see Dad's body. No one in my family knew how to help a young boy deal with his grief at the loss of his father and the sudden disappearance of his mother. Had hospitals allowed children in to see their ailing parents in those days, I might have been better prepared for his death. So what does the body do with unresolved grief? What does a child do with trauma? The energy gets locked inside the body. In my case, this led to life-threatening asthma attacks and panicky gasps for breath. Weekly visits to the doctor for shots in both arms went on for years in an attempt to stem extreme allergic reactions to pollen, dust, and who knows what else.

"Tommy, it's time to stop playing," my mother would say. "We have to go get your shots now."

I hated it all. Underneath the asthma and the fear lay stuffed emotions that exploded outwardly as testosterone hit when I turned thirteen, leading to a cycle of destructive juvenile delinquency fueled by alcohol. I was sad, angry, short-tempered, and wallowing in self-pity. I was running a story: "I got fucked over by my dad's death, so I am going to fuck the world over twice as much."

That story drove me to begin lifting weights to build up my skinny frame, so I would be strong enough to beat up anyone I might get in a fight with at school or in the street.

And fight I did. Given the right provocation, something would snap inside and my reptilian brain would take over with its fear-based conditioning to destroy the threatening other. My buttons were especially pushed when I'd been drinking, which was pretty much every weekend and sometimes during the week.

Twice, my opponent was so badly injured they had to be taken to the hospital. One of them might have died if the blood clot in his eye had gone to his brain. The other, suffering a concussion after a gang fight during which I pounded his head to the pavement of a back-alley street in Washington, DC, could also have died. Both hospitalized "opponents" recovered from the damage, sparing me from facing manslaughter charges.

It was a gift of grace that I was never caught for my most serious offenses, including burglary, car theft over a state line, and destruction of property. I was also privileged in that my skin was white and my parents (my mother married Ray Pinkson three years after the death of my father, Fred) could afford a good lawyer, so all I ever got was probation. Looking back, I realize I was divinely protected—I could have easily ended up in jail, or worse.

Another saving grace for me was spending time outdoors. Growing up in New York City had meant playing in parks, rocking on seesaws, digging in sandboxes, and roaming free in an empty lot beside our apartment building. I'd especially liked climbing on jungle gyms and swinging from the bars.

Being outside came to mean more when I was three and our family traveled to upstate New York for vacation. We stayed in a rented country home beside a small pool and a vegetable garden tended by caretakers who lived on the land. There, Mother Nature spoke to me for the first time, although I didn't understand it in that way at the time. This was my first journey beyond the city's confines, where the only untouched nature I was exposed to regularly was the occasional tree growing through a concrete sidewalk.

When my mother took me out to the garden on the day of our arrival, I was thrilled with the excitement of new adventure—there were new sights to see, smells to experience, and places to explore; I'd never seen a garden.

I don't remember anything about the walk to the garden, but I vividly remember being in the garden. It was a moment of epiphany, a doorway opening to a totally new and unexpected realm that transformed my understanding of reality. What took place in that little country garden so altered my notion of how things work that it remains with me today as a reference anchor, a centering point in my life, a navigational compass orienting me toward the miracles of nature and my need to be intimately in touch with its gifts on a regular basis for both my physical and mental health.

So what shocking, mind-blowing event happened in that rich, black earth amid bright red tomatoes, thick yellow squash and melons, green pods of string beans and peas, insects buzzing, and warm sunlight dancing lazily in the hot and humid August sun?

My mother walked me to the center of that lush and lively hotbed of growth, bent down to the ground, and pulled up a carrot. My eyes must have grown large with surprise. I don't recall if I had any awareness of what a carrot was before then, but that didn't matter because my mother immediately brushed the dirt off, dipped it into a bucket of water, then stuck it in her mouth and took a bite. I was shocked. *Stuff comes out of the Earth and you can eat it?*

I was transfixed. This was totally new for me. My only relationship with food up to this point was that it came out of our kitchen cabinet and refrigerator, so obviously those appliances were the source.

But something new and revolutionary was unfolding. The next thing I knew, my mother stood up and handed the carrot to me.

"Here, Tommy, take a bite," she said.

I hesitated at first, nervous. But it was my mother giving it to me, and she had done it first, so it must be OK. I looked at the shiny carrot, put it up to my mouth, and took a bite. A burst of energy exploded in my mouth. *Fantastic!* It was true! I could eat right from the Earth!

A few days later my mother took me out to the garden of wonders and showed me how to draw a two-inch-deep row in the dirt, the length of the garden. She picked up a small package, opened it, and shook out bits of something I had never seen before. She bent over the row and started dropping the small bits into the furrow. She handed me some bits and motioned for me to do the same.

"These are corn kernels, Tommy. They will grow into corn that we can eat for dinner."

It seemed pretty strange to me, but I followed her example. After all, I had already witnessed the amazing things that could happen in this new territory called a garden. She walked over to the hose and handed it to me, with instructions to hold it tight while she went to the spigot and turned it on. The next thing I knew, the hose buckled and cold water rushed out of the nozzle. I stood there, marveling at the water's force, when my mother ran over to take hold, giving me my first lesson in watering as she directed the spray to the newly planted seeds.

"The water will help the plants grow," she told me.

It sounded like magic, but I believed her. Equally important to me at that time was the action, power, and fun of watering.

I came out to the garden with her every day of our vacation to pick vegetables and, of course, to do my watering job. I could turn the water in any direction I wanted—what control, what delight, to see the sparkling, gurgling liquid make its mark on dirt, bushes, and plants.

One day as we entered the garden, I noticed little green shoots sticking up in the rows where we had placed the corn kernels. This was truly astounding. I don't know what I expected, perhaps fully grown cobs of corn such as I'd seen on my dinner plate. But no, this was something different. It was life itself coming up from an invisible underground I couldn't see.

Each day, I watched in amazement as the flimsy little shoots grew taller and thicker, reaching upward to the blue sky. We didn't get to stay long enough to see the corn grow to its full height, but one day, back in the city, Mother served us a dinner that included shiny cobs of rich, golden corn.

"These are from the garden, Tommy, from the seeds we planted. They are full grown corn now, and we can eat them!"

I was beside myself. Holding my cob and munching down into its juicy kernels was a double delight—a delicious tasty treat and a lesson in the Earth's ability to feed us.

My appreciation of the natural world grew deeper when, several years later, my mother, my younger sister Ilsa, and I moved to my grandparents' home in Southern California. The new environment helped ease the pain of my father's absence. I reveled in the year-round warm weather, playing at the beach, riding horses in dried up riverbeds, and watching tumbleweeds roll across open spaces that seemed endless. Every morning my grandfather would take me into the backyard, where a huge avocado tree grew. He would knock down avocados with a long stick—seemingly infinite avocados rained down daily at his poking into the branches. My job was to gather up the avocados and bring them into the house, where my grandmother used them in making our breakfast omelets. And so I learned that it wasn't just small plants that produced food.

Shortly after we arrived in Los Angeles my mother took me on a trip to Yosemite Valley. It was my first experience of mountains and wild animals, boulders bigger than houses, and cliffs taller than New York City skyscrapers. A deer ate out of my hand. A bear raided our tent in the middle of the night. I was thrilled.

Nightfall brought more gifts: stars shining brilliantly in the dark sky. I couldn't recall ever seeing stars back in the city, but here they were, pulsating points of light sparkling magically in the pitch blackness of a clear mountain night. They seemed to be winking at me. Maybe my Daddy was up there in that great immensity, winking at me too.

Towering mountains, waterfalls, animals, and huge redwood trees—I was in heaven.

I had the same feelings when my mother took Ilsa and me to visit the high desert of Palm Springs. The majesty of Yosemite and desert vastness breathed new life into me. Its majestic grandeur and wildness touched deeply into my wounded soul.

Today, I understand how these early childhood experiences in nature awakened a sense of awe and the impetus to adventure deeper into the power and beauty of nature.

Three years after our move to Los Angeles, my mother remarried and we moved back east to suburban Maryland where my new dad, Ray, had an electrical contracting business. Fortunately for me, our little brick house was next to woods and open fields. My favorite pastime, other than sports, was wandering those woods where I roamed throughout the seasons, creating imaginary adventures and enjoying my independence as a replacement for the freedom I'd had in balmy Southern California. Cold or hot, rain or snow, my love for being outdoors only grew stronger as I grew older.

Scientists have now proven that spending time in nature is good for our health, and can even measure how time spent in nature strengthens the immune system. I didn't know that then, but I was finding my path to healing within the wisdom of nature. My early encounter with death had plunged me into what mythologist Joseph Campbell calls "a hero's journey." I was on a quest, driven by a question I couldn't articulate at the time.

But now, in my late seventies, I recognize it clearly:

"In a world where death can come unexpectedly and take what you love most without asking your permission, is there anything that's truly worth basing a life on?"

CHAPTER 2

DEEPER KNOWING

Do not be conformed to this world,
but be transformed by the renewing of your mind.

ROMANS 12:2

B ryan was eight years old and bedridden with cancer. He'd been fighting a hard battle that included an amputation of one leg from the hip down, several lung surgeries, and intensive sessions of chemotherapy and radiation. Still, the cancer had spread throughout his body.

There was nothing else that could be done medically, so Bryan's parents had brought him home to die.

His mother told me he was upstairs, and probably wouldn't talk much because of the sedative effect of the pain-killing drugs he was taking. I went upstairs to his room. Bryan was lying very still with his eyes closed. The nearby TV was blasting away. I sat down beside his bed and greeted him. Several minutes went by as I sat in silence, watching his indomitable spirit struggle for breath in his pain-wracked body. Then Bryan opened his eyes and sat up. He could barely muster enough strength to adjust his pillow for an upright position. I leaned over to help him get comfortable.

He looked at me, suddenly clear-eyed and earnest, and asked, "Do they celebrate Christmas in heaven? And what about Easter—do they celebrate that too? Will there be a house for me there, like my house here?"

I was struck dumb by the suddenness and impact of his questions. I searched my mind for answers, but found none.

"What's it like to die?" he asked further. "Does it hurt?"

It was six weeks before Christmas, and Bryan knew he probably wouldn't make it to this important holiday. He'd miss celebrating with his family as he had all of his young life up to then. What was to come for this valiant little fighter, soon to die?

Bryan was one of many important teachers for me in my decades of working with people facing life-threatening illness.* Another young teacher, facing death at a similar life stage, told me: "Everybody has an assignment in life. That's why we're here, to work on it. Sometimes they're longer and sometimes they're shorter, like with me. But that's why we're here, to work on our assignment. And when we're finished, we get to graduate."

The experience of death, referred to here as "graduation," is a transition we all must face. It is the great equalizer. Unlike other times of transition in the life cycle, which might be ignored, repressed, or unacknowledged, death demands our attention. In my journeys and work around the world, I've noticed that death and dying is an open part of Indigenous peoples' daily lives. Shamanic cultures take their young people through rites of passage, such as the solitary vision quest in a wilderness setting that exposes the participant to death and the mysteries beyond. This empowers the kind of healthy respect for life and the gifts each person carries that we see too little of in our supposedly more advanced, technology-based society.

Psychiatrist Elisabeth Kübler-Ross, who famously described the five stages of grief, is quoted as saying that there are essentially only two human emotions: love and fear. In Western cultures, fear of death is often paralyzing and prohibitive, rather than connecting and inspiring. Fear is tied to the "fight, flight, or freeze" response, a physiological reaction that occurs during a perceived harmful event, attack, or

---

*Check out my book, *Do They Celebrate Christmas In Heaven?* (published by Wakan Press in 1998).

threat to survival. What feeds that fear is the belief that we're isolated, alone, separate from each other, and separate from nature. This belief is instilled in us from the time we are born. Childhood conditioning by well-meaning adults who also hold that belief continuously reinforces our view that we are separate entities, disconnected from all others, and should therefore be fearful of others.

Spiritual teachers, mystics, and Indigenous cultures around the world have been telling us for eons that this perception and belief about separation is not true.

Quantum physics, the study of deepest reality, now tells us otherwise.

"The inseparable quantum interconnectedness of the whole universe is the fundamental reality," says physicist David Bohm. "If we don't see this, it is because we are blinding ourselves to it."

Albert Einstein, too, understood the mistaken belief that we are separate: "A human being is a part of the whole, called by us 'universe' [. . .] He experiences himself, his thoughts and feelings as something separated from the rest—a kind of optical delusion of his consciousness."

Mainstream pedagogy holds humans as individual entities separate from others—separate from the Earth, the ocean, nature, plants, and animals. This has opened a doorway to doing whatever we want without having to consider the effect of our acts on others or the environment. Nature is seen as "out there" rather than a part of us, and we a part of nature.

This illusionary perception of a disconnected reality is the root cause of today's fear and existential angst. Spiritual teachers, mystics, and Indigenous cultures around the world have been telling us for eons that this perception and belief about separation is not true, that underlying the appearance of separation, we are all one. "Beware of the surface of things," advised *Mount Analogue* author and mystic René Daumal. In cultures such as ours, which place primary value on material acquisition and surface appearances, these voices usually go unheeded and are largely ignored.

All of what appears to be empty space is actually composed of particles and antiparticles dancing in and out of expression, which comprises an infinite field of vibrating energy. Different levels of energy express different informational downloads, but they are all an expression of cosmic intelligence that knows how to make and sustain a universe—perhaps even an infinite number of universes, as some physicists speculate.

As a kid growing up in Maryland before the advent of huge shopping centers, I did not know anything about the science of interconnection or the proven value of reflective time in nature. I just knew that playing in open fields, sledding in the winter, walking quietly in the nearby woods, wading in creeks, and watching deer, rabbits, birds, clouds, and trees swaying in the wind made me feel happy and gave me a great sense of peace. It still does to this day.

But my joy in nature didn't protect me from the reality of our "civilized" world. One day, as I was walking through the woods with a new friend, we came to a clearing with a tall wire fence around it. Inside were fancy-looking buildings, a big pool, and a sprawling golf course. It was a high-tone country club for the affluent.

A sign on the fence read, "No Dogs. No Colored. No Jews."

I was stunned. That meant me. My mother and two fathers, Fred and Ray, as well as my grandparents on both sides were all Jewish. My grandparents had emigrated to the United States in the early 1900s to escape the violent pogroms that periodically devastated Jewish ghettos in Europe. During one such attack, my great-grandfather on my mother's side was killed when he was thrown out of the second-story window of his home.

Although my new dad, Ray, occasionally pointed out neighborhoods that were off limits to Jews as we drove through the suburbs, my eight-year-old mind couldn't grasp it. What did "covenants," the ones that allowed only Caucasian Christians to occupy houses, even mean?

Although not religious, my parents lived the progressive Jewish tradition of standing up against oppression and injustice, just as our ancestors had done to gain their freedom from slavery in ancient Egypt. I grew up amidst political organizing and demonstrations for peace, justice, civil rights, and brotherhood for all people. My parents taught me that prejudice of any kind was a terrible thing.

Shocked by the sign on the fence of that country club, I froze. Systems are often developed from a fear response to others. I couldn't enter this place. I was not wanted. I was deemed not suitable. Every day in elementary school we were required to sing "America the Beautiful," which ended with the words, "and crown thy good with brotherhood from sea to shining sea." Some brotherhood! My antenna for being lied to grew to new heights.

In the fourth grade, I detected another untruth when we were supposed to be studying grammar, a subject I found extremely boring. I was spacing out, watching the tree branches moving in the wind outside the window, when suddenly, Mrs. Sims was standing over me, busting my reverie.

"You have to learn this or you won't be able to communicate!" she said with a glare.

I didn't say a word in response, but thought to myself, *That is totally not true. I already know how to communicate, so if she believes what she said is true, I have no respect for her. If she doesn't believe it is true and is still telling me it is, then I have even less respect for her because she's just laying something on me to get me to believe what we both know is bullshit.* It raised a big question in my mind: What other false information might school have imposed on me that I didn't notice?

That same year, I began to question "The Pledge of Allegiance." Initially, I had loved standing at attention each morning, facing the American flag, and reciting the pledge together with the other kids—especially those final words, "with liberty and justice for all." It made my heart swell. However, it didn't take me long me long, given the racism, discrimination, prejudice, and anti-Semitism I was now seeing around me, to conclude that those words were not true. Another lie.

I stopped automatically believing what I was being told by mainstream culture. Although pressured by my school and counselors to conform to their system, to do better, to live up to my potential—a potential that intelligence tests claimed I had in abundance—I felt like a square peg being hammered to fit into a round hole. I didn't like it, and so resisted.

I entered Kensington Junior High not long after the Supreme Court ruling requiring the racial integration of public schools. Unlike many of the other white students, I was comfortable with Black kids, having spent five years growing up in the Bronx. Black kids were among my best friends, and their parents were family friends as well. When we moved to Maryland, the secular Sunday school I went to had a brotherhood program with a Black church in Washington, DC The Reverend Dr. Martin Luther King Jr. preached there when he was in the DC area.

My junior high had a large number of Black students, most of them literally living on the other side of the tracks in a poor neighborhood just a few miles down the road from where I lived. Our kinship developed in the world of sports, my greatest passion at the time. When I was twelve, I played on the first integrated Junior League baseball team in the state of Maryland as one of two Caucasian kids on an otherwise Black team.

All this made it painful to hear white kids saying racist things when no Black kids were around, and contributed to furthering my alienation from mainstream culture.

Other than sports, junior high school was a total turnoff for me. I loved reading and was passionate about learning about whatever I was interested in. I read encyclopedias and history books for fun; but sitting inside at a desk all day, listening to teachers drone on about subjects I didn't care about was most definitely not for me.

Soon after the seventh grade began, my math teacher called me a name she thought was cute but that I didn't like. I called her a name back. She kicked me out of class and sent me to the principal's office, where the sadistic vice principal took delight in smacking troublesome kids with a wooden paddle with holes drilled in it, so it would sting more.

Not long after this incident, I started skipping school with older kids who did so on a regular basis. Trying to be cool like them, I also started drinking. We would stand in front of a liquor store and ask adults we deemed might be sympathetic to our cause to buy us beer. We gave them money, they bought the beer, then gave it to us in a back alley behind the store.

I also started drinking whiskey from my parents' liquor cabinet when they weren't home. At thirteen, I would get drunk and walk the neighborhood, looking for some kind of action. The action I found was usually throwing up. Unpleasant as it was, the drinking gave me a temporary release from a pain I couldn't name. Drinking and ditching school became a way to escape.

One day, after having skipped school for a few consecutive days, I was hitchhiking home, knowing I was going to be in trouble. I'd recently finished reading Jack Kerouac's book *On the Road*, and was fascinated by the characters' travels back and forth across the country. It sounded like a great adventure. Standing with my thumb out, I saw two friends going in the opposite direction.

"Hey!" I shouted. "Where are you guys going?"

They had skipped a few days of school and decided that, rather than going back to face the music, they'd run away.

"Want to come with us?" they said.

Fueled by a romanticized vision of the open road, I decided to join them. I went home to pack up a few things, and wrote a short note to my parents explaining my plan: "I have decided to run away from home. Do not worry. I promise to keep you updated on where I end up."

I met up with the other guys, and we decided to hide out in the nearby woods for a few days until the weekend, when an older friend could drive us out of the immediate area to where we could hitchhike without being recognized. We didn't really think about where we would go or how we would live. We just wanted to get away from what we knew, and taste the freedom we imagined running away would bring us.

Friends from school brought us food and told us there was an all-points lookout for us. We became outlaw celebrities of a sort, as more and more kids came to hang with us after school, and told us the latest news about how parents and the police were trying to find us. The weather was warm, so we slept without camping gear on the soft green of a nearby golf course, and headed back to the woods before dawn.

On the third day, I left the hideout to visit a friend. My dad, driving along the same street, saw me and stopped the car beside me. I ran off through an open field, hoping to get away. Ray gave chase, and caught me when I couldn't get through a barbed wire fence at the end of the field. Busted. He brought me back to the car and drove me home.

I expected fireworks, but he said only one thing: "Wait till you see what you did to your mother."

When we got home and I saw the depth of her distress, I was consumed with guilt. Running away had just been an adventure for me. In my teenage self-absorption, it never occurred to me that the note I left would cause such fear and worry. My mother had done nothing but support me, and she didn't deserve the pain I had inflicted on her. In truth, it wasn't her or my new dad Ray I was rebelling against, but a sociocultural worldview that was trying to force me in to a system and set of values I didn't believe in.

Looking back now, I recognize how I needed, and would have benefited from, a rite of passage. But that knowledge was not present in my mind, or in anyone else's I knew at the time. This unmet need for a testing adventure fueled my acting out delinquent behavior, with its risks and excitement of being caught.

My teenage years grew increasingly difficult. As admirable as my parents' values were, they didn't directly address the pain of my unresolved grief from my first dad's death.

Once, when I was angrily complaining about something, I was shocked when my mother said, "Tommy, you shouldn't feel that way." I was dumbstruck. *That's ridiculous,* I thought to myself. *First off, I already am feeling this way. Don't I have a right to feel my own feelings?! What do you mean, I shouldn't?* From that point on, I knew it wasn't OK to express my upset feelings, so I pushed them down further within, creating more pressure and more suffering.

Nature, though, remained my refuge. One afternoon, wandering aimlessly through the woods near our house, I lay down on the ground in an open patch among the trees. Lying still, I felt the soft earth, the warmth of sunlight, heard the soft wind rustle the leaves. I closed my eyes and relaxed. Suddenly, I saw myself at the bottom of a twelve-foot hole, a hole I had dug myself and was digging deeper through my self-destructive behavior. I looked up to the sky and realized that, to get out of the hole, I had to accept what I considered the injustice of my dad's death, along with the hypocrisy and injustice I saw in the world. I didn't have to like it, but I had to accept it as part of life. I had to create a different response to the world and to my loss, because if I didn't, the hole would just get deeper, with increasingly disastrous outcomes. I had to change, but I knew I didn't have the inner strength to do it while living in Maryland. My whole identity, my status, came from being a tough guy you didn't want to mess with. I had to get away to where no one knew me and I could start over.

Things went downhill in my senior year, when my girlfriend's parents put their foot down, refusing to let her go out with me. They cited my drunken behavior, which they had witnessed a time or two when I brought her home from a date.

That was the last straw. I remembered my vision in the woods, and planned with a close friend—a fellow member of a gang a handful of my fellow alienated teenagers had started in eleventh grade—to run away together. We decided we were going to quit school, take off to California, work until we were eighteen, then go to junior college and apply ourselves to making a fresh start in a new locale.

Somehow, my mother found out about our plan the night before we were going to take off, and came to my bedroom. "Tommy, I know you are very unhappy now, and that you want to leave. I know what unhappiness is like, and I am so sorry you feel the way you do." She looked at me with tear-filled eyes. "Dad and I love you, and we believe you can turn your life around if you want to. You are intelligent and, underneath your behavior, a good person." Even though I was frustrated with the life I was in and wanted to leave home immediately, I heard her out.

"If you stay and finish your senior year," she said, "Dad and I will help you out financially to go to California and start your life over again."

She told me how hard it had been for her when my dad, Fred, had died, but that she had made it through that time and rebuilt her life, and now it was working again.

We made a deal. My cheeks wet with tears, I agreed to not run away, and to finish my senior year. It was a torturously long, long semester and I hated it. At times I went to school drunk. More fights, more truancy, more acting out, but I kept my part of the deal and made it to graduation, though I barely passed. In a haze of drunkenness, I walked up to receive my diploma—a piece of paper that held no meaning for me.

My post-graduate education is a long story that I will go into later in this book, the sum of it being that five years after graduating from high school, I graduated from San Francisco State with a degree in sociology, and two years after that I graduated from U.C. Berkeley with a master's degree, and some years after that I graduated from the Saybrook Institute with a Ph.D. in psychology, where my doctoral work was based on the Indigenous vision quest tradition and a successful Wilderness Treatment Program I started at a drug program called Marin Open House.

One of the people on my doctoral committee was Dr. William Lamers, who had also been the medical director of the drug program. Toward the end of my doctoral program I asked him what kind of people he thought I would work with best.

"People that are dying," he said.

I was shocked and taken aback. "Why? What does death have to do with my wilderness and vision quest work?"

"People who are dying are on a vision quest, though they may not see it as such. They are searching for deeper understanding and connection to help them face their dying process," he said, "and you have been leading quests with addicts to help them find connection to a strength that can help them heal their addictions."

Although his suggestion felt right intuitively, I questioned whether I had what it would take to meet the demands of working with the dying. The confidence I'd gained from my recent success with the Wilderness Treatment Program did not extend to this new arena.

Bill invited me to teach a class with him on death and dying, through which I could explore for myself the possible relevance between what I knew from the Quest work in the wilderness and those who were physically dying in their homes and hospital beds.

At the end of the course, Bill suggested that I join a project he was involved in—a group designing a hospice program. Once again I was fearful to take on the task, but guidance on a vision quest gave me the confidence to proceed.

I began to visit dying people to offer my support. Mainly, though, I listened. I listened to their fears, their hopes, their life stories. What struck me most was that those who believed in some power greater than themselves, whether it be God, nature, or the cosmos, were more likely to reach a sense of peace about their coming death as well as have a higher-quality experience leading up to it. Those who did not have a belief system beyond ego identification were more likely to be fearful, or angry and depressed.

While the hospice program we started—the first at-home program in the United States and only the second of its kind—was doing an admirable job of addressing the physical and psychosocial needs of patients, meeting their spiritual concerns did not get the same kind of attention. It was not a comfortable arena for the volunteer group of doctors and nurses who comprised our initial staff. I started to get frustrated because it was the spiritual needs of the people I was assigned to visit that I felt best suited to work with. I wanted to address those needs, despite the rest of the staff's discomfort with the topic.

Around that time, I was introduced to Dr. Jerry Jampolsky, a psychiatrist who had started the Center for Attitudinal Healing to provide group support for children with life-threatening illness. Jerry asked me to join his staff, and I gladly accepted because the principles of Attitudinal Healing that Jerry explained to me were based on a nondenominational spiritual foundation of unconditional love.

Jerry and I worked together for over thirty years, and grew very close, to the point where I called him my spiritual older brother. Our love for each other deepened and grew until his death in 2020, shortly after a warm, loving visit at his houseboat home on the San Francisco

Bay. I miss him, and carry his love and teachings deep in my heart. Working with Jerry and the principles of Attitudinal Healing provided a framework for meeting life challenges, which I use to this day.

It was Jerry and our work together that led me to Bryan and the gift of an ongoing mission to share the good news of our essence as divine beings of a love that never dies.

The Twelve Principles of Attitudinal Healing

1. The essence of our being is Love.

2. Health is inner peace, healing is letting go of Fear.

3. Giving and receiving are the same.

4. We can let go of the past and of the future.

5. Now is the only time there is, and each instant is for giving.

6. We can learn to Love ourselves and others by forgiving rather than judging.

7. We can become Love finders rather than fault finders.

8. We can choose and direct ourselves to be peaceful inside regardless of what is happening outside.

9. We are students and teachers to each other.

10. We can focus on the whole of life rather than the fragments.

11. Since Love is eternal, death need not be viewed as fearful.

12. We can always perceive others as either Loving or fearful and giving a call of help for Love.

◆ *The Past that Feeds the Present*

We go through our days with a socially conditioned notion of reality running through our minds and running our lives. Does that reality paradigm serve you or limit you? Find a comfortable spot to relax in. Take some deep breaths to slow down, calming your mind and opening your heart. Consider the following questions, reflecting on how your past influences your present.

+ What life events in your childhood had the most impact on you?
+ How did you respond to them?
+ What story did you create about them?
+ Is that story still influencing your life today?

The power to change only comes when we face and accept our realities.

CHAPTER 3

EXPANDING REALITY

The best and most beautiful things in the world cannot be seen or even touched but must be felt with the heart.

HELEN KELLER

The lines on the wallpaper next to my bed began to move as if they were alive, as if they were breathing, undulating in waves that swept across the entire wall. I was totally mesmerized . . . A material object, wallpaper, was behaving as if it were alive. How could this be?

I was ten years old and not in a drug-induced state, but suffering a high temperature from a viral infection the doctor said was a precursor to polio, which, thankfully, I did not get. What I did get was my first psychedelic experience, which opened my mind to an expanded understanding of reality; there was more going on than I had known previously, something really mysterious induced by an altered state of consciousness. My mind raced:

What is reality? What else exists beyond the ordinary state of consciousness?

The road to answers opened up after high school. I left Maryland to start afresh in Southern California, drawn by fond memories of the three years I'd spent there after my father's death. The open spaces, the warmth, the absence of gnats and humidity, and the year-round outdoor lifestyle were irresistible.

On reaching Los Angeles, I enrolled in junior college, working part-time to fund my stay. My first year there was dedicated entirely to academics. There were no parties, no bars, no dating. I was there to prove to myself and to others that I was not a failure. My routine consisted of studying, working, and going to the gym to lift weights, a regimen I had begun four years earlier. The discipline and concentration required for weightlifting also reinforced my mental resilience, a strength that bore fruit when I made the Dean's list and was invited to join the school's honor society.

Besides proving to myself that I could succeed academically, the next best thing about junior college was meeting Andrea Csillag Danek.

Andrea was a Hungarian refugee who, along with her family, had escaped following the tumultuous 1956 revolution. This period, marked by violence and chaos, resulted in the deaths or injuries of thousands. Andrea, who'd been just eleven years old residing in downtown Budapest, bore witness to these tragic events. One day, she went to the movies with her younger sister, who was only four, just a couple of weeks after the uprising against Soviet rule had begun, with Hungarians firmly resolved to liberate themselves from the oppressive Soviet dictatorship. Upon exiting the theater, the sisters were confronted with a terrifying sight: Soviet tanks rolling menacingly down the street, firing indiscriminately at anyone they came across. Acting swiftly, Andrea guided her sister to their parents' location, and from there they hurried home. They were fortunate to have survived the violence physically unscathed, but the emotional trauma of witnessing such brutality and narrowly escaping was deeply etched into Andrea's psyche, a haunting memory she would carry with her for life. I am forever grateful that she lived through this ordeal.

Seeing Andrea walking around campus for the first time, I felt an immediate attraction. I made up my mind to meet her after spotting her circling the football stadium in an open Cadillac, as one of the school's homecoming queens.

During my second year of junior college, I began to loosen the iron grip on my social life. I joined a fraternity and started attending their parties—parties that Andrea's sorority also frequented. We met at one such gathering, and began dating.

In several ways, Andrea and I were quite different. She was raised Catholic and her family was part of Hungary's affluent social elite. Vali, Andrea's mother, was a renowned prima ballerina who performed internationally and acted in films. Andrea's father, Alphonse, was a successful industrialist who owned multiple large chemical factories in Budapest. I later discovered that he had saved hundreds of Jews during the war by providing shelter for them in his buildings. He'd been imprisoned and physically abused at one point, but fortunately was released after several weeks.

Andrea's family held a strong anti-communist stance, a sentiment that stemmed from the brutal Soviet occupation of Hungary under Stalin and the violent suppression of the freedom fighters during the revolution Andrea had witnessed.

In contrast, my parents were progressive, working-class individuals with socialist leanings. They had struggled during the Depression and were actively involved with labor unions, fighting for better conditions for workers. Andrea, on the other hand, was politically cautious due to her experiences with Soviet communism. As for me, I was a rebel, pushing against authority and challenging the hypocrisy and materialism of mainstream capitalist-consumer values.

Despite these differences, we shared strong values when it came to family, children, honesty, animals, integrity, and the pursuit of enjoyment. We were a couple throughout my last two years at junior college.

Another beauty caught my eye one weekend, when I visited a cousin attending U.C. Berkeley, but this one wasn't a person. It was the San Francisco Bay Area itself. Having never been to Northern California, I was transfixed by the Bay, the hills, the cable cars, North Beach, and remnants of the beatnik scene. I decided to apply to San Francisco State, got accepted, and moved there in the fall of 1965. Despite the distance, Andrea and I continued dating via frequent phone calls, letters, and visits between

San Francisco and LA. The separation, surprisingly, helped our love grow stronger, and the next summer I returned to LA to be with Andrea and work as a neighborhood organizer protesting the Vietnam War.

My arrival in the Bay Area for college introduced me to a whole new way of living. In the fall of 1965, the Bay Area was in the initial throes of a psychedelic-fueled insurgency. Originating in the Haight-Ashbury district, what came to be known as the Hippie Movement began pushing back against conventional social norms, and eventually spread around the world. San Francisco State was a hotbed of radical exploration and expression.

This is not Los Angeles, I thought to myself my first day on campus, as I observed the hippie attire worn by many of my fellow students. The pages of a new chapter in the book of my life were unfurling before me. *I need to open up to this and see what happens.*

Meanwhile, the war in Vietnam, a conflict I deeply opposed, was escalating. Having done my research, I knew that our reasons for being in Vietnam were not based on noble causes; we were there to protect and benefit our own political and financial interests. Prior to arriving at San Francisco State, my political involvement had been limited—my most notable experience being in 1963, while home for the summer from my first year at junior college. I had marched with my family to hear Dr. Martin Luther King Jr.'s iconic "I Have a Dream" speech at the Washington Memorial. However, at San Francisco State I found an outlet for my rebellious, truth-seeking spirit. I joined the Vietnam Day Committee and assisted in organizing demonstrations around the Bay Area.

With the draft looming, the prospect of being sent to Vietnam was a threat I had to confront. Determined not to go, I sought help from the Quakers, who offered counsel on various methods to avoid the draft. Together, we devised a plan to use the asthma I had suffered from as a child, presenting it as a still-active medical disability. If this plan failed, my backup was to escape to Canada. Fortunately, the asthma strategy worked, and I was deemed medically unfit to serve in the armed forces.

The fear and uncertainty of being drafted eventually subsided, allowing me to continue my college journey. I chose sociology as my major, excited to finally delve in to the classes I had initially signed up for—those focused on understanding the human mind, behavior, and societal interactions. I hoped these studies would shed light on my turbulent high school years and maybe even equip me to assist young individuals grappling with similar challenges.

My professors, quintessential radical thinkers deeply embedded in the Bay Area's zeitgeist, consistently challenged mainstream perspectives. They posed thought-provoking questions, one of which led me to reassess my previously held beliefs about marijuana. I had been taught that smoking marijuana would inevitably lead to heroin addiction. However, a social psychology instructor assigned a book that unveiled marijuana's usage by artists, musicians, painters, poets, and intellectuals to stimulate their creativity and enhance their sensitivity. I came to realize that the world wouldn't collapse from smoking weed; another "truth" I had accepted crumbled.

Life during the late sixties and early seventies in the San Francisco Bay Area was an immersion in a renaissance of exploration and questioning. Over time, I discovered that some of my professors were conducting research on lysergic acid diethylamide (LSD), which was legal at the time. This piqued my curiosity. Classes in psychology, sociology, and social psychology had stimulated my interest in delving in to the power and mysteries of the unconscious mind, beyond the threshold of the ordinary waking state. From the stories I heard all around me, it was clear that LSD was a powerful tool for exploring exactly what I wanted to learn more about: the deeper contents and processes of the mind.

LSD fascinated me, but also frightened me. The media was rife with sensational stories about the alleged dangers of taking LSD. However, the fact that respected professors were conducting research with it reinforced my belief that it could be responsibly used for beneficial outcomes.

For an entire year, I devoted myself to reading and learning all I could about the effects of LSD. I confronted my fears about the potential horrors hiding in my unconscious mind that could surface if I took LSD.

During a creative writing class, our instructor divided us in groups and issued an intriguing directive—we were not to discuss the past, only the present. I was astonished at how challenging it was to remain solely in the moment. The same professor also led us on a field trip to San Quentin prison, where we protested against an imminent execution. On a regular basis, my limited ways of thinking were being confronted and expanded.

In all the research I read about LSD, I gave little attention to the spiritual experiences that many individuals reported. I was a staunch atheist, under the belief that religion was for the feeble minded, easily manipulated by the fear of a wrathful God. One of my professors brought up a famous quote by Karl Marx: "Religion is the opiate of the masses." This sentiment resonated strongly with me. My interest lay solely in LSD's potential to unlock the doorway to the unconscious—I was in pursuit of genuine truths.

◈ Your Turn

- Do you ever question your unconsciously conditioned beliefs about life and about reality?
- What do you no longer believe to be true that previously you didn't even question?

CHAPTER 4

OPENING MINDS

The real world is very different from the misshapen universe they have created for themselves by means of their culture-conditioned prejudices.

ALDOUS HUXLEY

The water, infused with powdered LSD, held an unfamiliar taste. I emptied the glass to its last drop.

The year was 1966. My three companions, trustworthy and seasoned by their experiences, encouraged me to heed John Lennon's advice from a popular Beatles song of the era: to silence my mind, relax, and imagine myself floating downstream. I reclined in the safety and comfort of my Haight-Ashbury second-story apartment, prepared to embrace whatever came next.

Roughly forty minutes later, an array of swirling colors began to dance on the white stucco ceiling. My rational mind, grappling to maintain its conventional mode of understanding, proposed, *These could be microscopic specks of color that are ordinarily invisible, but the LSD might be magnifying and distorting them.*

As the reds and blues, the greens, yellows, and oranges started to blend in to undulating shapes, I released a lengthy outbreath and let go. I ceased trying to rationalize the unfolding spectacle, stopped attempting to control the experience, and surrendered to the potent current sweeping me away. The moment I did so, the swirling patterns overhead sprung to life in an entirely new manner. The ceiling transformed to a cinema screen. Mesmerized, I observed a cycle of ancient Meso-American life unfurl. There were scenes of couples making love, babies being born and breastfed, children at play, then growing up, teenagers and adults laboring in the fields, aging, passing away, and the arrival of new life in the next cycle. These images spanned across countless epochs.

All of it felt strangely familiar, as though observing a scene from a previous life. A voice from deep within declared, *"Not only did you live during this era, but you will return to it again in this lifetime. It isn't something to pursue or seek. Carry on with your life. The right time will bring it to you."*

Gradually, the vibrant panorama began to dissolve. I lay there, entranced by the spectacle I had witnessed.

Before I had a chance to digest everything, a new energy pattern started to reveal itself on the undulating ceiling. *Now what?* I pondered. *"Inhale, exhale, let go once more. Allow it to unfold. You're not in control,"* a voice in my head instructed.

Once again, a sort of time vortex unfurled. The fresh scene depicted a lengthy procession of people, extending from the present back through the epochs to the dawn of humanity. Gradually, I realized I was witnessing my ancestral lineage journeying through time. Each generation imbued the next with its experiences, all the way up to my parents passing their experiences on to me. I perceived how each generation built upon the wisdom it had received, shaping its worldviews and values, before progressing to the next generation. This cycle continued through the ages leading up to my birth, molding my beliefs, my values, my self-perception, and my understanding of reality.

Beneath the eons of ancestral conditioning there lay an unchanging true essence, a light-filled energy interconnected with infinite cosmic consciousness, unified with all of creation. At this level of being, there was no separation, only interwoven oneness. I understood then that ego identity was akin to an ocean wave perceiving itself as a separate entity, forgetting that while it had its unique form and individual expression, it was, in reality, part of the larger entity—the ocean itself. Under the influence of LSD, I perceived how my ego identification as Tom Pinkson was a mental creation, and that my physical body was a time-space container housing a portion of energy connected to an infinite energy field.

As a child, I'd often laid on the grass during humid Maryland nights, gazing up to the sky and trying to comprehend what a friend's father, a scientist, had told us while driving us home from school: "The universe is infinite. It never ends."

I'd pondered, *How could that be? There has to be an end to everything.* I tried imagining venturing out into the sky as far as one could go. Surely, there would be an end somewhere? But if there was an end, what lay beyond it? My mind simply couldn't grasp the concept of infinity. It felt as if the attempt was causing my brain's wiring to short circuit.

Now, in the psychedelic, LSD-induced state of non-dual consciousness, I was able to grok infinity. "Grok," a term coined by science-fiction writer Robert Heinlein, represents the complete comprehension and understanding of something.

My third LSD trip, in 1967, led me to a deeply unsettling and confrontational experience about existence in this universe as a human being. This trip, in stark contrast to my earlier ones, propelled me into a state of consciousness where I found myself floating alone through the boundless expanse of cold, empty space, utterly devoid of spirit, love, or anything meaningful.

I was terrified. The fear of being eternally trapped in this emptiness began to take hold. I questioned, *What if there truly is nothing "out there"? What if existence truly lacks any meaning?* I was swept away by an overpowering wave of dread and depression. But then, a thought surfaced: *What if I confront and accept the idea that life and the universe are indeed meaningless? What then?* I pondered over this for what felt like an eternity. The depression, sadness, and fear deepened.

Then, another thought emerged: *If there is no inherent meaning, I am free to create my own!* This prompted me to reflect on what held true meaning for me. The answers came swiftly: love, kindness, caring, and heartfelt connection. *Well then,* I thought, *that is what I am going to create! These are the values that will bring meaning to my life.* I resolved to live by these values, infusing meaning into the seemingly barren emptiness of space.

The moment I made this decision, a cosmic curtain lifted and brilliant light obliterated the darkness. I felt elated, blissful, and fortified—enlightened. I recognized that my decision to create my own meaning was the key that unlocked a door I hadn't even known existed.

I felt empowered and inspired to Live Love as best I could, and I have been striving to walk the path of love ever since. When I falter, succumbing to toxic reactivity, I strive to embrace my human frailties and perceived shortcomings with compassion, tenderness, and love. This way, healing love can flow to the places it's most needed.

My father's spirit visited me during a psychedelic journey, aiding in bringing healing energy to a part of me that was deeply wounded and lost—the little boy who never got to mourn his father's departure from his life. I hadn't truly confronted my long repressed grief. It had been pushed down into the depths of my unconscious shadow, adversely affecting my physical and mental/spiritual well-being.

Fred's spirit communicated, "I know how hard it was for you to lose me when you were so young. But you need to understand that my love for you never died. It merely transitioned beyond the confines of a physical entity. My love is here for you now and always, unbounded by physical limitations. This is a lesson about love that you needed to learn. It will serve you and enable you to help others as you proceed with your life. I love you."

These words enabled me to forge a new narrative—a life-affirming story that replaced the resentful, self-pitying, life-constricting old tale I had clung to for so many years.

Psychedelics dramatically opened my mind to an expanded experience of reality. From this state, I clearly witnessed how I had constricted my life's possibilities by believing that the totality of my being consisted of the time-space container of my physical body and its ego identity. What I'd been told and thought to be true due to cultural conditioning—that we are separate entities existing in a universe of separate identities and objects—was not true. I had been deluded, tricked by the smoke and mirrors of external appearance.

At the deeper levels of being, there is no separation, no division—only blissful oneness, with access to infinite creativity. *Ah, perhaps this is what underlies the notion that we are made in God's image.* This new understanding of reality strained my rational mind's ability to comprehend. Yet, it somehow also felt familiar, as if returning to a place once known but forgotten. The Huichol Indians have a word for this kind of knowing: *iyari*, or heart memory.

The door-opening power of the psychedelic experience helped me see how my use of alcohol produced an effect opposite to what I was now experiencing with the aid of LSD. Alcohol constricted consciousness; LSD expanded it. In that moment, my relationship with alcohol changed. I'd have a beer or margarita once in a great while, but that was it. Why dull a consciousness capable of experiencing such magnificence?

Grasping infinity would have been quite enough for me, but the LSD was not yet finished with its revelations. A new swirling of energy began to manifest on the ceiling. This time, I found myself amid a crowd of people. Roman soldiers, both on horseback and on foot, were struggling to keep the crowd under control as people jostled for a better view of three men being crucified. Compelled, I too moved closer.

To my shock, I saw that one of the men was Jesus. As soldiers drove long, thick nails into his body to secure him to the cross, he shuddered in agony with each impalement. Witnessing his fate, I shuddered with empathy.

In a split second, my awareness leapt out of my body and entered that of Christ's. I could feel his pain as if it were my own. Anger and thoughts of revenge surged from within me. I desired to kill the men inflicting the torture.

Then, I heard a voice—Christ's voice. It shook the very foundation of my being. "Forgive them, Father; they know not what they do."

In that moment, a kind of love I hadn't even known existed flooded into me. This love held no anger toward the soldiers driving in the spikes. Quite the opposite. From Christ's heart, love poured directly into the soldiers' hearts.

"They are asleep," he seemed to be saying. "To punish them will serve no purpose. They are hurting themselves and do not even know it. They are like unconscious children crying out for love."

Quite unexpectedly, I burst into tears of joy. I felt the power of a cosmic energy field of infinite, unconditional love. My anger couldn't hold. My "tough guy" stance couldn't hold. In that moment, I understood how people around the world carry Christ in their hearts as a spiritual being with the healing power of love as his essence. This level of consciousness was embodied in the values I'd grown up with, in a secular Jewish home that emphasized kindness, honesty, caring, generosity, sticking up for the underdog, and justice and equality for all people. My Christ vision held all of these qualities in the form of a spiritual energy force of infinite light, love, wisdom, and compassion.

I came down from the acid trip in a daze, but totally determined to learn how to stay in connection with and thereby understand the overwhelming love I had experienced. I wanted to find out if I could replicate the state I had been in without using LSD.

Acid heads around me told me that the way to understand the altered state of consciousness was to study Eastern religion—Hinduism, Buddhism, and Taoism. I signed up for Eastern religion classes at San Francisco State, and read the Bhagavad Gita, the Upanishads, and other sacred Hindu texts. I learned about sages who spoke of how the "manifest" realm of objects, forms, and human beings is continually being born out of the formless "unmanifest." Atman, the Godhead within, and Brahman, the God presence without, were both of the same essence.

What I experienced in my first LSD journey is referred to in Vedanta Hindu scripture as a *samadhi* experience. Patanjali, the ancient Hindu sage and author of the two-thousand-year-old book *How to Know God*, characterizes a samadhi experience as a higher kind of transcendental knowledge.

The physical realm does not encompass everything; there is an underlying reality beneath it all.

Psychologist Charles Tart would classify the three numinous visions I'd had as "state-specific information." Tart suggests that human beings possess numerous different channels of perception, each containing distinct energy frequencies operating at various levels of consciousness, with information unique to each channel. Different cultures nurture and cultivate different channels.

Predominantly, Eurocentric culture emphasizes intellectual information derived from rational, logical, and linear-based channels. Anything outside of this is often dismissed as mere dream, imagination, or nonsense, thereby undermining the value of information from alternative channels.

My experiences with LSD opened a visionary channel that tapped in to what British botanist Rupert Sheldrake refers to as "morphogenetic fields." These fields contain energy information that exists in time and space. However, similar to gravity, they are invisible to the naked eye in ordinary states of consciousness. The physical realm does not encompass everything; there is an underlying reality beneath it all. But, because we cannot perceive it in our usual state of consciousness, it often elicits fear, leading to a reluctance to acknowledge and validate it as a credible source of valuable information.

I read and studied ancient Chinese sacred texts, especially the Tao Te Ching, which emphasizes living in harmony with the universe's flow. It advises learning how to align with the flow rather than resisting it, avoiding it, or trying to control it. There was much to flow with right in my neighborhood.

At that time, Haight Street and the Bay Area offered a smorgasbord of yogis, swamis, and storefronts serving up various Eastern teachers and teachings. I attended yoga and meditation classes and retreats, learning practices from masters that I continue to this day. My life was transforming. Instead of focusing solely on changing the world through political activism, I now wanted to change my inner world as well. I continued protesting the Vietnam War, the racist exploitation of migrant farm workers, and racism against People of Color, but I also became a full-fledged hippie. I let my hair grow long and wore psychedelic clothes that reflected the colors and feelings of my visions. Throughout it all, though, I stayed grounded enough to remain in school and earn my degree in sociology.

Andrea and I married in the summer of 1967 and moved to Berkeley, where I had been accepted into the University of California Graduate School of Social Welfare. I knew I wanted to help people, and starting a private practice in counseling seemed the most likely route: The social work program at Berkeley would take just two years, as opposed to the three years of a graduate program in psychology. Besides, society's welfare was a major concern of mine, and I hoped the two years would help me become more skillful in my social justice work as well.

We found an apartment near campus, and I started my classes while Andrea secured a job at a bank to help finance my studies. My time at Berkeley was nothing short of adventurous. We were constantly surrounded by protests of various kinds. Student activists and hippies seized control of People's Park, a parcel of land owned by U.C. Berkeley originally slated to become a parking lot, and transformed it with furniture and art. It quickly became a battleground between the police and protestors, resulting in numerous injuries and even the death of an innocent bystander watching from a nearby rooftop.

A different kind of battle unfolded on campus when my fellow students and I went on strike, demanding the inclusion of classes focused on Black, Indigenous, Latino, and Asian history and perspectives in the curriculum. Our protests against the war in Vietnam also persisted. At times, Berkeley resembled an occupied city for weeks on end, with soldiers patrolling the sidewalks, tanks lining the streets, and tear gas permeating the air.

I was right in the thick of it all, both excited and scared. On more than one occasion, I had to flee from the police, whom we derogatorily referred to as "Blue Meanies" due to their blue uniforms. They wore black masks to protect themselves from the tear gas they fired at us while charging with shields and billy clubs.

I interned as a parole officer with the California Youth Authority as part of my graduate studies. My supervisor arranged for the release of Black kids who had fallen into trouble and landed in jail, assigning them to me. I picked them up from jail and took them to the Black Panther Party office in East Oakland. There, they could foster a sense of Black pride and involve themselves in activities that were beneficial to the Black community, rather than those that were detrimental to themselves and others.

With the Panthers, I distributed free food to needy families. My childhood experiences made me feel at home working with both young and old Black individuals. During my summer construction work jobs, which I started at the age of fourteen, I found myself mostly in the company of Black men who shared my indignation about the pervasive racism and hypocrisy of mainstream culture. In some ways, I felt more at ease with Blacks than with whites. None of us bought in to the narratives we were being fed about American greatness, as we were individuals who had endured discrimination, violence, and prejudice.

One morning, I woke up to the news that several Black Panthers had been killed in a shootout with the police the previous night. One of them was the man with whom I had made food deliveries just a day earlier. We had planned to continue this work the following day, but for him, that day never came.

The local papers initially blamed the Panthers for the violence, but it was later revealed that Attorney General John Mitchell had orchestrated a deliberate plan of violence against the Panthers. This plan included media manipulation designed to portray the Panthers as a threat to mainstream society.

The reality, however, was quite different. Huey Newton and Bobby Seale founded the Panthers with the intention of protecting Black lives from the rampant violence regularly perpetrated by racist officers in the Oakland Police Department.

Feeling that students and teachers at the graduate school needed to be aware of the atrocities being carried out against Black people in the streets of Oakland and San Francisco, I delivered a passionate speech during my first year at Berkeley. I criticized the school for its failure to address these immediate realities.

This speech resulted in my election as vice president of the graduate student body, a position that tasked me with organizing school events and inviting speakers. Since the school was not addressing these pressing issues, I decided to bring these issues to the school. One of the guest speakers I invited was Kathleen Cleaver, then-wife of Black Panther Eldridge Cleaver, who penned the bestselling book *Soul on Ice* while incarcerated in San Quentin State Prison.

I was on a quest to integrate social activism with my newfound understanding of the importance of inner work. I made a presentation to a graduate class about the responsible use of LSD as a tool for broadening consciousness and accessing a wider reality. My interest lay in this expanded reality: how to access it, attune to it, learn from it, and utilize its wisdom to navigate the challenges of everyday life.

CHAPTER 5

HONORING THE FEMININE

I bring you the ancient women's mystery stories.
Take the time to listen to me.

SUSAN S. WEED, *MENOPAUSAL YEARS:*
THE WISE WOMAN WAY

Today, a growing number of individuals around the world, both men and women, are working to honor the feminine, the cosmic Goddess. This trend is partially attributed to the increasing popularity of a psychedelic brew—ayahuasca. Used ceremonially by Indigenous people of the Amazon for thousands of years, this psychoactive concoction, once confined to shaman-led ceremonies in the heart of the Amazon, is now gaining widespread use globally.

Often referred to as The Mother, Mother Aya, or Grandmother, ayahuasca provides a conduit to the spiritual intelligence of the feminine wisdom flowing from nature—the maternal force from which we all originate.

This dark brown, typically bitter-tasting liquid is a meticulously crafted mixture of a specific vine and certain DMT-containing flowers. These ingredients are boiled for extended periods in water, while serenaded by the shaman throughout the preparation process. Indigenous people of the Amazon believe that the vine embodies masculine power, while the flowers channel feminine energy. Together, in a respectful, cooperative partnership, they form a sacred union. This harmonious interplay of male and female plant spirits presents a paradigm for human behavior. In response to the challenges of our times, it's no coincidence that The Mother is offering her healing assistance.

In my early efforts to learn about Indigenous spiritual traditions, an elder once told me, "You're too full of yourself. You need to humble yourself. You need to open yourself to your feelings and to your intuition." These qualities are usually associated with the feminine but are also accessible to the masculine when not suppressed or denied.

To successfully navigate the waves of life and meet these challenging times, we need to embrace both the masculine and the feminine in a cooperative, respectful working relationship—a sacred marriage within ourselves.

The beginning of dismantling my macho conditioning occurred with my first LSD experience. Until then I'd been a captive of patriarchal conditioning, despite the early influences of my mother, Ruth; my grandmothers, Sarah and Ella; my aunts, Marion, Mary, Rose, Ida, Eva, and Mildred; and my sisters, Ilsa and Briane.

The psychedelic perceptual lens helped me discern the toxicity of the machismo cultural brainwashing I had completely absorbed out of fear and ignorance. This fear stemmed from a worry that in my vulnerability I might be exposed as something other than the tough guy persona I tried to present to the world. My visionary experience of the consciousness in Christ that allowed him to show compassion for his persecutors led me directly to the existence of a field of infinite, unconditional love consciousness. This revealed itself as the underlying reality of existence—the essence of who and what we all are at the core of our being. This expanded mystical state of non-dual reality, recognizing the underlying oneness of creation, is what I refer to when I say "psychedelic."

When I came down from the power of my transformational journey, I knew I wanted to embody this newfound awareness of love in all my relationships. This included my relationship with the feminine, setting me on a path to acknowledge this attribute within myself and to appreciate and support its flourishing in others and the world. This endeavor meant unlearning the toxic aspects of male dominant history and immersing myself in her-story, the untold and suppressed narratives of historical oppression and violence against women and the feminine wisdom.

I started to delve into all the resources I could find about goddesses and sacred priestess figures from around the world. In Taoism, a religion that emerged in China thousands of years ago, ancient sages emphasized the significance of the feminine, the yin, which yields and merges with the flow of the Tao. In ancient Greece, the feminine is represented through the concept of Gaia, the Mother Earth Goddess. The Kabbalah, an ancient Hebrew mystical path, also identifies the divine feminine with Shekinah, which means "in-dwelling" and refers to the presence or soul of God that accompanies us. When you experience God's presence, Kabbalists say, it is actually the Shekinah, an aspect of God and a Divine Being in her own right.

Jungian studies introduced me to the concept of the anima, the repressed and often dishonored feminine aspect within men. Through my readings I discovered how cultures of ancient Europe were based on egalitarian, matrilineal, and matriarchal structures, sharply contrasting the patriarchal paradigm of domination prevalent in what author Thom Hartmann refers to as "younger cultures."

Like most Western men, I was raised in a culture that emphasized domination through physical power and force. Growing up in the 1950s and early 1960s, the model of masculinity was a tough, independent, self-controlled man who took no nonsense from anyone and showed no signs of vulnerability. This was considered the epitome of a "real man." The absolute worst insult for a young man was to be labeled a wimp, seen as weak or vulnerable, to cry, show "softer" feelings, or be dominated by a woman. The only times vulnerability ever surfaced and softer feelings emerged for me were when I drank enough to drown my defenses in alcohol. However, this path did not lead to healing; it was a toxic trap that wreaked havoc on my emotional and psychological health.

Working toward creating a sacred balance between my masculine and feminine energies helped me realize the significance of utilizing male strength to create a safe space for the feminine voice to be heard and respected.

As I began to learn about the Indigenous spirituality of the Americas, I saw and experienced firsthand how feminine wisdom was vitally important to the survival of our species here on Mother Earth. Spending time with Native people allowed me to witness respect for feminine wisdom in action, instead of just reading about it. A significant portion of this learning came through time spent with Rolling Thunder (RT), a medicine man I first encountered when he visited Haight-Ashbury.

I later met RT at a powwow, and received an invitation to visit him and his Shoshoni wife, Spotted Fawn, at their desert community, Meta Tantay. This visit meant adhering to the customs of the Shoshone during our time at the camp. Women experiencing their menstrual cycles, their "moon," stayed in a tipi with other women in the same phase, and were visited only by other women. They were relieved of household chores, work, and parental duties, except for nursing babies. The moon lodge was a time for reflection, prayer, listening to dreams, and engaging in creative activities of their own choosing, while allowing their natural flow to enter the Earth to fertilize it for new growth.

The women were sequestered away from men and the larger community, not because they were considered dirty or unclean, but because they were recognized as being more sensitively connected to the powers of the universe during this time. This was quite a different understanding of a menstruating woman than what I had learned from growing up in mainstream America, where menstruation was often negatively referred to as being "on the rag."

Throughout my years interacting with Indigenous people worldwide, I learned that a moon lodge practice was commonplace. Women were revered for their heightened spiritual attunement during this time and for their ability to bleed without succumbing to death.

My stay at Meta Tantay, where life was closely tied to nature and each day was filled with gratitude prayers, storytelling, and lessons about medicine from a respected elder, felt incredibly sane. This new awareness of menstruation as a sacred time for women led me to conduct an all-night honoring ceremony around a sacred fire when my daughters reached their first moon time.*

Working toward creating a sacred balance between my masculine and feminine energies helped me realize the significance of utilizing male strength to create a safe space for the feminine voice to be heard and respected.

A dream I had during solo time on a vision quest underscored the importance of masculine energies in valuing and protecting the life-nourishing gifts of the feminine. Not long after, I had the opportunity to put this insight to practice.

The last night of the quest, I sat before the fire with fellow questers as each shared their experience of solo time. The lone woman in our group spoke last. She had been working on healing childhood trauma. She shared how a song had come to her that had been of immeasurable help in her process, but she didn't want to sing it for us because she feared it might sound hokey. Forewarned by my dream, I offered her my support.

"Sister Suzette," I began, "I believe the song you received was not only given to you for your healing but also through you for others. I invite you to sing it for us with the understanding that it is a sacred medicine gift. By offering it to us, you honor yourself as a Sacred Woman and bless us with your sharing. If this doesn't feel right to you, I accept that. You need to do what is best to take care of yourself. Still, I offer the invitation."

I leaned back to allow her space for her response. For long minutes, she gazed intently into the fire, a worried look on her face. I was curious to see what she would decide. The fire crackled, the wind moved softly

---

*For more on this, you can read my essay, "Honoring a Daughter's Emergence into Womanhood," from the book *Fathers, Sons and Daughters*, edited by Charles S. Scull.

through the night. Slowly, she looked up and started to sing. It was soft at first, but her voice gained strength and volume as she continued. The tenderness of her song touched us all. By the time she finished, several of the men were in tears.

"That was beautiful," I said. "Thank you for your courage in bringing it forth. It is a medicine song, a power song that needs to be sung. You have been gifted with something that is *wakan*—sacred, in the language of the Lakota. Carry it out to the world, for it will help others in their healing as it has helped you, and touched us all very deeply."

In the years to come, I was fortunate enough to spend time with medicine women from different tribes, each of whom helped me understand more about the power of the feminine and deepened my appreciation for its life-nurturing and life-protecting wisdom. The domineering model of patriarchal rule has brought us to the brink of ruin. To survive, we must embrace the wisdom of the feminine and foster a sacred marriage with the masculine. Neither is superior to the other; both are essential in forging a cooperative partnership of equals, working together in harmony and balance.

The journey from my initial machismo-based identity to one embracing feminismo has been long. I have been richly blessed in this growth through friendships with many wise women, particularly older grandmothers in their eighties, who have been inspirational examples of living life to the fullest. My daughters Kimberly and Nicole have also been excellent teachers, as they have grown to be strong women unhesitant to correct me when necessary, and offering their wisdom when they see I need guidance. My greatest teacher in fostering this growth, however, has been my relationship with Andrea, my life partner for over half a century.

Andrea and I considered ourselves a couple soon after we started dating, but in the 1960s hippie abandonment of the mores of straight society, I was not interested in getting married.

That is, until one day, while sitting on the floor of my rented apartment going over materials for an anti-war demonstration I was helping organize, I heard a loud, authoritative voice in the empty room.

"You are already married to Andrea on a soul level. That will always be true whether you honor it or not. In fact, you were married before in a previous life." The voice came through with a power of truth, and I decided then and there to honor its message. I called up Andrea.

"We're getting married. Let's go down to the Justice of the Peace and make it legal."

Andrea was stunned but happily agreed, and we were married the next day, with her pleased parents and sister as witnesses.

Later that summer, we had a marriage ceremony back East for my family, then returned to LA and got married a third time before family and friends on the West Coast. We chose a rose ceremony conducted by Brother Bhaktananda at the Self Realization Fellowship Lake Shrine, founded by Paramahansa Yogananda. My best man, Nick, made pot brownies that I and other members of my male entourage enjoyed prior to the ceremony. It was a beautiful ceremony, enveloped in the love of those close to us.

The word "love" is used in so many different ways. Through movies, novels, and personal experience we all have our notions about Eros and romantic love with sexual attraction. In contrast, platonic love is love for friends, parental love for children, familial love for brothers and sisters, grandparents, aunts and uncles, and cousins.

Agape love is expressed through kindness, tenderness, care, generosity, courage, perseverance, responsibility, and integrity. It is compassionate, empathetic, and seeks Win-Win resolutions for the greatest good of All. This is not a superficial, Hallmark card kind of love, where one ego loves another ego. Agape love serves the soul.

When we channel our thoughts and actions to agape love, we become stronger, healthier, more powerful, more vibrant. We light up. Conversely, when we indulge in self-critical judgmental thoughts about ourselves or others—judgments that deny our true identity—our hearts close, our energies become stagnant, our immune systems weaken, and we experience emotional, psychological, and spiritual suffering.

A clear intention to strengthen our relationship and underlying love, coupled with prayer, meditation, and reminding myself of the mantra

"I am love and my love is for giving," has been immensely helpful in overcoming my own ego reactivity patterns. I had plenty of opportunities to practice this intention through disagreements that arose between Andrea and me as we delved deeper into our marriage.

After one particularly upsetting argument, I realized that framing our marriage in a spiritual context could assist me in navigating difficult times, especially when my self-righteous and stubborn ego blamed her for the discord and fantasized about leaving. I prayed to the feminine energies within me, asking for assistance in letting go of masculine control and avoidance patterns, and for help in softening my heart to channel the love energy my psychedelic journeys had shown to be the most crucial part of existence. The softening did occur, the love did prevail, and today I have Goddess statues and altars in my home and yard to which I express my daily gratitude for their continued assistance in living the love that I know I am. Each day, I connect in prayer with Goddess energy, praying for her wisdom, guidance, and strength in my daily life.

Regarding the increasing interest in ayahuasca usage worldwide, I find it fascinating that this psychedelic brew derives its potency from a sacred union of the masculine energy of the banisteriopsis vine and the feminine energy of chakruna flowers. This gift from the Indigenous people of the Amazon, a lens-opening gift of plant intelligence from the feminine Mother Earth Goddess, not only brings healing and attunement with her wisdom ways, but also imparts the teaching of the evolutionary importance of sacred union on all levels of our being. This understanding is vital to the development of Psychedelic Shamanic Wisdom Warriors, who hear the call and rise to the occasion, working to transform a fear-based paradigm of reality to a love-based one through which we cannot just survive, but thrive.

Toward that end, it might be beneficial to reflect on your attitudes and beliefs about masculinity and femininity and the quality of the relationship between them. Do they hinder or block the fullest realization of who you are as a human being? If so, what needs to be discarded so that you can move forward to the highest and most integral expression of your soulful self?

As for the difficult times that can arise in relationships with others when entrenched unskillful reactive behavior patterns are triggered, consider asking yourself the following questions, which I have found helpful in breaking patterns and reopening a closed heart:

- Do I want to be right? Do I want to win? Do I want to feed my ego identity and let it run the show?
- Or do I want to grow my relationship in a healthy Win-Win way based on cooperation, compassion, kindness, consideration, and love?
- How might I remind myself that I am more than my ego, more than a body that changes with time, more than beliefs and stories that reinforce separation and suffering?
- What practices help me move beyond ego and connect with higher consciousness remembering that I am love and right now is the only time I can give and receive it?

STEP TWO

Wise Up

Pull the plug on the unconsciously conditioned
thoughts and behaviors and co-create
with the divine creative wisdom power of the Universe,
a conscious relationship to the truth that
you are a Sacred, Worthy, Luminous Being,
that you are love and that your love is for giving.

CHAPTER 6

INITIATORY RITES

The period when the youth is at the verge of their conscious
individual life [. . .] should enter into personal relations
with the mysterious power that permeates and controls
nature as well as his own existence.

OMAHA ELDER, *THE SACRED: WAYS OF KNOWLEDGE,*
SOURCES OF LIFE BY PEGGY V. BECK,
ANNA LEE WALTERS, AND NIA FRANCISCO

The trail to the lake that would serve as our basecamp was approximately four miles away, if one were to fly straight there as a crow does. However, trudging at the age of seventy-six with a heavy pack on my back, my journey was far from the crow's effortless flight. Instead, it was a series of dragging steps, following a gurgling creek through forests of aspen and pine, with towering mountains flanking either side. We had started at an elevation of 6,463 feet, and the climb ahead would take me another thousand feet higher. The altitude was already making me lightheaded, wobbly, and weak.

This experience was a far cry from how it had felt in 1972. That was the year I first guided people on a vision quest, inspired by the Indigenous medicine people of North America. For forty-nine years, I had been honoring the elders who had initiated me to a lineage thousands of years old, handed down through generations. As a Caucasian *gringo*, I do my best to serve as a bridge builder between cultures and mindsets, a task assigned to me by my spiritual Huichol grandmother, Guadalupe. Long before I heard the term "global warming," Guadalupe explained that *Tayaupa*, Father Sun, was drawing closer to Mother Earth to awaken the gringos in the North because we had forgotten that the Earth is alive, and that the fire, the sky, the rain, and the wind are all living entities. We had forgotten how to live in a respectful, balanced way, which was causing problems for everyone. Vision questing is a powerful way for those of us in the North to reconnect to the divinity of nature, a keystone of my spiritual practice, which I share with others in support of their waking-up process.

On this particular quest, as I struggled physically, several younger, stronger questers offered to help carry my heaviest gear. I gratefully unloaded my bear-safe canister and we began our hike. Progress was slow. We paused as needed, which became more frequent as we gained altitude. It didn't take long for exhaustion to set in.

Stop. Rest. Drink some water. Consume energy snacks. Hike a few hundred more yards, then stop to rest again. Like an impatient child on a long car journey, I kept wondering: *How much farther until we get there?*

We hiked on at a turtle's pace. Pain throbbed in my legs, hips, and back. My breathing was labored. *OK, I get it. This is part of the vision quest medicine, part of purification,* I think. The challenge lies in accepting the suffering without letting it overwhelm me, in finding a way to appreciate being alive in this moment, in these beautiful mountains, even though physically I am a wreck. An inner voice whispers, *"Be grateful you are here, that at your age you can still do this. Remember, you are not your body, your feelings, your thoughts, or your exhaustion. You are Spirit. Live, love, now. It is the only time you can. Be fully present for each rise and fall of every footstep. You can do this. Call on Spirit, call on the strength of these mountains to help you keep going.*

"A Wisdom Warrior uses everything to grow in the ways they want to grow. You want to be more peaceful, more joyful, more loving. Do it now while under this stress. Dissolve your ego's attempts to feel sorry for itself. You are not your ego, so go deeper. Don't try to do it on your own. Connect with Great Spirit's strength to help you get to basecamp."

I almost made it. A hundred yards from basecamp, my calves cramped up in retch-inducing pain. If I took another step, I'd collapse. Grace arrived in the form of one of the younger, stronger questers who, having already arrived at basecamp and unloaded his pack, had hiked back to help me, taking my pack. What relief! Grateful, unburdened by the extra weight, I regained strength after a brief rest, and stumbled the final distance. I try to set up my tent but noticed that my mind and body weren't working well. Some of my cylinders weren't firing. I sat down, leaning against a granite boulder, to just be for a while. I drank water and pulled a Cliff bar out of my pocket.

Gradually, my body's electrolytes came back to balance, and I assembled my tent, unfurled my sleeping bag, blew up my sleeping pad, and flopped down, utterly spent and exhausted, but here. I'd made it, as the Beatles song says, "with a little help from my friends." It had been a literal, physical rite of passage over the miles from where we had parked our cars and started the trek. It was also an emotional, mental, and spiritual rite of passage through suffering to reconnection to Spirit and release into the peace of Its presence.

There are specific times of passage throughout the human life cycle, such as puberty, marriage, childbirth, menopause, and death. In traditional cultures, these transitions have ceremonial rites that provide support for the individual undergoing the change. When such rites are absent or lack meaning, people may suffer in solitude, but it is society that ultimately pays the price. The void left by these missing rites is often filled with unconsciously created behaviors, many of which are unfortunately destructive. The teenage years, particularly in America, are often marked by self-created boundary testing and pushing the limits with irresponsible drug taking, sexual behavior, and reckless driving. The high rate of overdose from opioid usage among young people serves as a prime example of an unhealthy attempt at a passage rite.

Older, more traditional societies have culturally supported rites of passage that guide initiates skillfully to new stages of their lives—times that can be very unsettling and disruptive without such rites. The vision quest is one such time-tested rite of passage that can induce a psyche-delic consciousness without the use of psychoactive substances.

My entry to the experience of spending solitary time in nature as an initiatory rite began in 1971 when I was hired by the California Outward Bound School to coach forty-five of their teachers in working with teen-agers and drug use. At the time, I was the treatment director at a drug program, Marin Open House, which I started with Dr. Roger Smith, a criminologist. My experience working with the Outward Bound teachers brought me face-to-face with one of my greatest lifelong fears: heights.

We were in Yosemite Valley, one of the most spectacular climb-ing spots in the world, for a ten-day mountain climbing and whitewa-ter river running training session for Outward Bound teachers from around the United States. I had never engaged in either activity before.

While I loved the mountains, heights terrified me. As I walked to the base of a granite cliff that rose straight up into the sky, I was over-whelmed with anxiety. I found myself praying for rain, or even for a minor accident like a sprained ankle, anything that could prevent me from facing the monstrous mountain looming before me.

I trembled as I looked up at the towering heights, with a certainty so absolute that it left no room for doubt—it was impossible for me to climb this sheer, cold, unrelenting rock face. Perhaps the Outward Bound instructors could do it, but not me. There was no way.

However, by the end of the day, after a morning spent learning climbing and safety skills and then making the ascent, I found myself standing atop a peak that my mind had previously convinced me was impossible to reach.

In that moment of exultation, I recognized with a sense of sadness how often I had allowed fear and negative thinking to limit me in life. Time and again, these factors had prevented me from attempting some-thing I wanted to do, simply because I was afraid of failure.

From that point forward, I made a vow to myself: I would no longer let fear hold me back. I wondered about the opportunities and accom-plishments that might have been possible in the past, had I not been too frightened to try.

My time with the Outward Bound instructors involved backpacking in the High Sierras and enduring twenty-four hours of solo time without food. Both were unfamiliar and intimidating activities that triggered significant anxiety and fear.

To my surprise, my LSD experience came to my rescue. Under its influence, I had perceived everything, even inanimate objects like rocks, as vibrant, radiant energy. Everything I looked at seemed to undulate with life, with consciousness, with being. The prospect of spending uninterrupted solo time fasting while immersed in nature could be an ideal opportunity to delve in to this vibrancy and explore my newfound sensitivity without using any psychoactive substances.

My campsite was nestled in deep woods, encircled by trees of diverse shapes, colors, textures, and sizes. As I leaned back into the support of a sturdy trunk, I began to observe the distinct characteristics and personalities of the trees spread before me. Tall, short, young, old, slender, thick, with trunks varying from brown to yellow, and some blackened by lightning strikes—despite their differences, they all shared a commonality: roots anchored deep into the Earth, with armlike branches extending outward.

It gradually dawned on me that the trees were imparting lessons on how to live a fulfilling life. The entities I came to call Tall Straight People grew straight upward, reaching toward the light of the sun, their branches outstretched as if in reverent prayer. They were simultaneously grounded, with roots firmly planted, yet flexible enough to sway and bend with the forceful gusts of the winter Sierra storms.

This seemed a wise way to live: root in Mother Earth, rise tall but stay flexible, and reach out to the light with gratitude.

My admiration for trees deepened when I learned about research by botanists revealing that trees communicate with one another, fostering robust cooperative communities that safeguard and support individual members. Pheromones disseminated through the air serve as warnings of pest threats. Complex interlaced root systems transport nutrients. Forests provide wisdom teachings about cooperation, pointing us toward creating communities that can offer greater resilience against the threats that surround us.

My initial experience in Yosemite was so powerful, it inspired me to embark on another wilderness solo the following year with a mountaineering friend. We joined together for the trek into the backcountry, only to go our separate ways for a more extended period of solo time and fasting.

Psychologist and wilderness quest leader Bill Plotkin, in his book *Soulcraft*, likens solo time to being in a chrysalis state within a cocoon, tested and threshed by boredom, hunger, cold, fear, loneliness, and withdrawal from digital stimulation and daily addictions such as coffee and sugar.

Threshed I was, indeed. Upon returning home, I came across a book called *Lame Deer: Seeker of Visions*. It told the story of a Sioux medicine man who'd completed a solo as part of his tribe's rite of passage for adolescents, initiating them to responsible adulthood. This was my first encounter with the term "vision quest." For the Sioux, solo time was more than just a wilderness adventure, as Outward Bound posed it, it was a spiritual rite of passage to expanded consciousness.

The Sioux tradition fascinated me because both of my solo times had led to spiritual communion experiences. While my study of Eastern mysticism and religion had served me well over the years, I now sought to learn about the spirituality of the land where I was living, and the ceremonies of the Indigenous people who had inhabited this land for millennia.

I set out to find an Indigenous Native American teacher who could guide me through a vision quest. I found one, surprisingly, in the guise of an art teacher at a junior college. Before he began sharing Indigenous wisdom, I had to humble myself and learn to listen. One teacher led to another as I continued to show up with humility and an open heart. Every experience with a medicine elder was an entry to the unfamiliar. I never knew what would happen, but I trusted in the wisdom that stretched back for millennia.

Throughout my life, I call on that wisdom to meet day-to-day life challenges, which I understand are actually opportunities to examine, dismantle, and dissolve the ego-identified patterns that created my suffering and open to greater consciousness than ego.

This process of inner work wove a tapestry I could not have anticipated, leading to work with shamanic Indigenous elders in settings as varied as high deserts, dense forests, thick jungles, high mountains, and

INNER TRADITIONS
BEAR &COMPANY

Inner Traditions • Bear &Company
P.O. Box 388
Rochester, VT 05767-0388
U.S.A.

PLEASE SEND US THIS CARD TO RECEIVE OUR LATEST CATALOG.

Book in which this card was found _____

❑ Check here if you would like to receive our catalog via e-mail.

Name _____ Company _____

Address _____

City _____ State ___ Zip ___ Country ___

E-mail address _____

Please check the following area(s) of interest to you:

❑ Health   ❑ Self-help   ❑ Science/Nature   ❑ Shamanism
❑ Ancient Mysteries   ❑ New Age/Spirituality   ❑ Ethnobotany   ❑ Martial Arts
❑ Spanish Language   ❑ Sexuality/Tantra   ❑ Children   ❑ Teen

Please send a catalog to my friend:

Name _____ Company _____

Address _____

City _____ State ___ Zip ___ Country ___

Phone _____

Order at 1-800-246-8648 • Fax (802) 767-3726
E-mail: customerservice@InnerTraditions.com • Web site: www.InnerTraditions.com

exotic islands around the world. Now, as I head toward my eightieth year, a grandfather three times over, I increasingly think about my responsibilities to the next generation. I remember the wise words from Bear Heart, an Indigenous elder who emphasized the importance of "teaching children how to live before teaching them how to make a living."

What can I offer that might be both meaningful and beneficial to my grandsons, Corbin, Luke, and Sebastian, as well as to other young individuals as they navigate the challenges of an increasingly precarious world? Reflecting on the significance of rites of passage in my life, I began to contemplate the creation of rites for them. I envisioned rites that could not only foster their growth but also effectively guide their reintegration to society. These rites would provide a socially recognized affirmation of their evolving roles and associated responsibilities. Today, we witness modern, diluted versions of these rites of passage in events such as birthday parties, wedding ceremonies, retirement celebrations, and funerals. However, I aspire to offer something more profound, something that would challenge participants to their core, thereby facilitating the graceful relinquishing of the old while confidently embracing their new phase of life, bolstered by a heightened awareness of their identity, nature, and life purpose.

A traditional rite of passage is composed of three stages: separation, liminality, and integration. In the first stage, the individual departs from their customary roles and duties, leaving the familiar to transition to the second stage—the liminal stage, where trials occur and rigorous challenges serve to break them down. Rites of passage test endurance, self-control, courage, and faith, aiding the initiate in learning how to manage anxiety and fear by establishing a connection with the spiritual realm. Upon the completion of the liminal stage, the initiate transitions to the integration stage. During this phase, they return to their normal life, incorporating their newly acquired state of being to their daily existence.

If the use of sacred plants were legal, they could be incorporated into adolescent rites of passage to adulthood. These rites could be facilitated by guides trained in the dynamics of such practices, as in many Indigenous cultures. This would be a much safer alternative than the dangerous experimentation with drugs that young people often undertake on their own, without the guidance of knowledgeable elders to educate them on the safe and responsible use of these substances.

This is especially crucial for teenage boys who need to learn how to channel the power of testosterone in a way that benefits their community. In the absence of these rites, this energy can become destructive. Evidence for this lies in the number of mass shootings committed by young white males in our culture, as well as their alarmingly high suicide rates.

The urge to create meaningful rites of passage for my three grandsons was further fueled after meeting Maladoma Somé, an African shaman, and reading his book *Of Water and the Spirit*. A mutual friend introduced me to Somé shortly after he first arrived in the United States.

Somé said that traditional education in his tribe addresses three areas:

Expansion of one's ability to perceive a broader reality.
Destabilization of the rigidity of habits tied to a single plane of existence.
The capability to traverse trans-dimensionally and to alter modes of awareness depending on the task at hand.

In his culture, wisdom elders have an "irreplaceable function in the life of the community. Without them, the young are lost, their overflowing energies squandered in futile or perilous pursuits. The old must exist within the young like a grounding force that reins in the inclination toward bold but senseless actions, and guides them on the path of wisdom."

The first initiation ceremony for the boys of Somé's people takes place when they are ten years old, and the second when they are thirteen. Inspired by this, I decided to create a rite of passage for each grandson when he turned ten. This rite needed to foster a connection with nature and the Earth, and to fortify their inner strength and capacity to confront fear without allowing it to deter them from living fulfilling lives. It needed to be an experience that would prompt them to tap into a power larger than themselves that they could seek assistance from in challenging times. These experiences would also aid them in discovering their unique gifts and ways to share them with the world, thereby contributing to making it a better place.

I sought guidance from the mystery of dreams. It was granted. I designed a series of rites of passage beginning when my grandsons turned ten, followed by another at thirteen, and the final one at sixteen. When the time came for each boy, they invited a few friends, along with their parents, to an orientation meeting.

TEN-YEAR-OLD'S RITE OF PASSAGE

In the meeting, I provide an overview of the concept of a rite of passage, emphasizing that it was not a fun getaway camping trip. Instead, it would be challenging and demanding—a test of their fortitude and courage. I clarified what they could anticipate and what they needed to do to earn the right to participate.

I emphasized to the ten-year-olds that, for the first decade of their lives, their choices had mostly minor consequences. However, in the next decade, they would be making decisions affecting not only their futures but also the lives of others. They would be making choices about their education, their driving habits, their handling of sexuality, and their consumption choices— what they chose to eat, smoke, drink, or inhale. They would also be deciding on the values by which they would live the rest of their lives. The quality of their lives would evolve from these choices, so prudent decision-making was paramount as they transitioned to the next ten-year cycle.

I assigned the boys four tasks to demonstrate their readiness and earn their right to participate:

Task 1: Identify the qualities of mind and character they aspired to cultivate in order to grow to be the kind of men they envisioned themselves to be.

Task 2: Construct a prayer arrow, sharpened at one end and with feathers on the other, bound in yarn of colors chosen to symbolize the qualities they sought to nurture.

Task 3: Compose a description of the qualities they wished to develop and forward it to me, along with an explanation of their motivation to undertake this journey.

Task 4: Finally, do an anonymous act of kindness for someone without being seen.

Each of the boys successfully met the requirements.

We initiated the rite at sundown, bidding farewell to parents and family members who had gathered in the parking lot near the trailhead of a natural park to see us off. We hiked to a nearby campsite situated at the base of a towering ridge that separated us from the Pacific Ocean. Each boy was equipped with a sleeping bag, a backpack, water, and some snacks. No tents were brought; only tarps were used for shelter.

We arranged our sleeping bags in a circle around a central altar I prepared with an abalone shell and some sage. After sharing our intentions, I steered the conversation toward the fear and anxiety the boys had been discussing among themselves. We explored various strategies to manage this fear, including breathwork, visualization, and mindfulness techniques. Then, we laid down for a few hours of sleep beneath the starlit sky.

At midnight, we roused ourselves, packed our gear, and embarked on a long twisting ascent up to high ridge. Our plan was to embark on a five-mile hike across its crest and descend the ridge at dawn the next day. The parents would be waiting at the base, eager to witness their sons plant their intention arrows where the sea kissed the shore. Each boy would declare their intentions aloud for all to hear, stepping forward one at a time to plant their arrow.

The night hike was carried out in silence, with flashlights only used during our rest stops. At one juncture, the entire group halted and Greg, the other adult accompanying me, ventured farther down the trail, disappearing into the inky darkness.

I informed the boys that he was somewhere ahead, but the exact distance was unknown to us. The rite of passage was about to become a more formidable challenge. Each boy, in turn, would walk off alone into the night, journeying through the unknown until he caught up with Greg, who would be waiting for him.

The thought of venturing into the dark night not knowing the distance to Greg filled the boys with apprehension. After all, they were well aware that mountain lions, coyotes, and rattlesnakes inhabited these hills.

We huddled together, brainstorming ways to summon courage in the face of fear. We discussed how to tap into a power greater than ourselves, drawing it from the earth beneath us and the sky above.

Before each boy embarked on his journey, we placed him in the center of our circle and showered him with support and encouragement for his upcoming "solo walk of fear." Some needed extra support to venture alone into the shadows, but in the end each boy summoned the courage required for the test and they all succeeded.

The next morning, after a night of hiking, we descended from the ridge to the ocean. The boys carried a new energy with them—a newfound confidence and sense of pride in what they had accomplished, both individually and as a group.

THIRTEEN-YEAR-OLD'S RITE OF PASSAGE

For my eldest grandson's next rite of passage, I took ten boys—the original group plus a few more new additions—all thirteen years old, on a three-day rite of passage to adolescence. This time, the boys had a series of ten tasks to accomplish to earn the right to participate in the passage rite, which I presented several months in advance at an orientation meeting with their parents.

The rite involved backpacking to a wilderness area, setting up a basecamp, sitting in a ceremonial circle around the fire sharing intentions, hopes, and fears for the test coming up, and then spending twenty-four hours alone in solitude with no food and no digital devices.

The next morning, without breakfast, each boy set out to the place of power that had called them. They would return to basecamp the following morning, having spent a full cycle of day and night alone, facing their fears by themselves.

That night, thunder and lightning filled the skies. Because we were in the high mountains, I was concerned for those boys who had chosen more exposed sites, rather than lower down in the forest. I had to work my faith and trust muscles, keeping strong protection prayers going for the boys, then surrendering them to Spirit's hands.

I eagerly looked forward to reuniting with them the following morning, hopeful that each would show up safe and sound. They did return, in good shape and brimming over with stories. They were also famished, so we broke our fast together after a short thankfulness prayer. Each boy shared what they were thankful for, breathed their gratitude into a pinch of tobacco I had given them, and then placed it in the fire.

Later that evening, around the campfire, each boy shared what had tested them, how they coped with it, and what they discovered about themselves.

Upon our return home, we held another ceremony with the boys' parents and families. The boys narrated their experiences from the quest, and what they had learned from it. Similarly, the parents shared their fears and hopes about having their sons venture off into the wilderness alone, and the emotions it evoked in them. Quite a few parents expressed their wish for a similar rite of passage back when they were entering their teenage years.

A thanks-giving potluck dinner marked the end of what had been, fortunately, a successful adventure for everyone involved. I was filled with a sense of gratitude and relief.

SIXTEEN-YEAR-OLD'S RITE OF PASSAGE

Three years later, when they were sixteen, some of the boys who had heard me talk around the campfire about my six-day vision quests approached me, expressing their desire to undertake this longer quest.

"This will be a much more challenging test," I warned them. "Two full days and nights alone, fasting, in the Sierra Mountains."

Although a few of the boys had scheduling conflicts due to sports camps and family vacations, six of them committed to the longer quest. Upon returning to basecamp after their solo time, each boy echoed a similar sentiment: "It was the hardest thing I've ever done!"

Here's an account of one boy's experience:

The world intimidated me. It was full of unknowns, potentially unpleasant experiences. I was scared of not finding my place in it. I feared what lay beyond the places I had already traveled. The enormous adventure of leaving home was daunting.

When I was ten, my best friend wanted to celebrate his birthday with a coming-of-age ceremony led by his grandfather, a shaman. Together with our friends, we hiked through the night, braving the unknown, the darkness. I found a thrill in the natural world. At fourteen, he proposed another ceremony. This time, we went backpacking and fasted for thirty-six hours. Our aim was to gain a deeper understanding of our own lives and how to live them to the fullest.

We agreed—we wanted to embark on a full vision quest. This would involve two full days and nights away from basecamp fasting during solo-time, No entertainment whatsoever—just myself, the natural world, and my thoughts. At a time when I was struggling to define my identity and ground myself in preparation for the next chapter in my life, I was eager to seek clarity amidst my confusion, fear, and hesitation. I viewed the vision quest as an opportunity for deeper self-discovery and personal growth.

The essence of a vision quest is to alter one's typical living environment to induce a state of heightened introspection. However, during my solo time, it wasn't the fasting that was most challenging. It was the absence of human connection, the lack of the people I love. I found myself reflecting on the supportive community I have around me; the love that would always be there to catch me should I fall.

Upon completion, when I considered everything I had endured, I realized I had accomplished something incredibly difficult yet rewarding. I had experienced extremes—hunger, loneliness, and discomfort—but I had persevered. I made it through. The realization dawned on me that I can achieve anything I set my mind to. I understood that I am strong enough to face the world, not just because I am capable as an individual, but also because I am supported by a loving community.

I am strong enough to face the world because I am loved.

Alone in the wilderness, I found myself contemplating all the elements that make life joyous and effortless for me. I reflected on the countless individuals worldwide who confront daily struggles, who might never know the comfort and love I've been blessed with. It hit me then, with a clarity as sharp as the mountain air, just how profoundly thankful I am. I am grateful for the roof over my head, for the love I receive, and the love I can give. I am thankful for the clean water that flows from my tap each day, the food that graces my table, and all the other seemingly mundane things that shape the quality of my life. I recognized, in that moment of solitude, just how fortunate I truly am.

The world, with its vast unknowns, can be a frightening place. Yet, these unknowns have led and will continue to lead to personal growth. I didn't know what awaited me in the mountains, but I confronted it, emerging stronger.

I've realized that fear is only detrimental if it paralyzes me from facing what I dread. True courage lies in pushing through that fear. I've discovered that I understand myself well, and I possess all I need to succeed. I've learned to identify what is truly important to me and understand that one can never really express enough appreciation for what many people take for granted. Now, I am ready to face the world.

You may not find yourself in a life situation that allows you to develop a rite of passage for others, or to embark on a personal vision quest into the wilderness. You may not have the opportunity to travel to exotic locales to learn from Indigenous elders. However, you can choose to Wise Up at any moment, simply by spending time in the natural world with humility, receptivity, and an intention to learn.

Select a location in nature where you can be still and relatively undisturbed by other humans. This could mean hiking into the woods or finding a secluded field, or it could be as simple as sitting in your own backyard.

Once you've settled, take your socks and shoes off so the bottom of your bare feet touch Mother Earth. Let her energy flow into you. Relax your body and calm your mind with slow, deliberate breaths. With each exhalation, express gratitude for being alive and for the life that surrounds you: the trees, bushes, flowers, the Earth beneath you, the sky above, the air you breathe, the gentle breeze, the spirits of the place, the animals that share this space, the ancestral spirits of the Indigenous people who once inhabited this land, and all that you can see and appreciate, both visible and invisible but nonetheless present.

◄ Pay attention to whatever catches your interest.

◄ Breath in peace, harmony, and joy.

◄ Breath out and release whatever needs to go.

◄ Open your heart.

◄ Pose a question and let it float in the air.

◄ Sit still and be with your breathing, enjoying with gratitude whatever the spirits of the place bring to your awareness.

◄ Listen within and ask yourself: Is there anything you feel called to do in your life but are afraid to act on?

◄ Ask the expressions of nature where you sit if there is anything they could give or show you that would help you follow through on your calling.

◄ When it's time to end and return home, give thanks to the spirits of the place.

You may or may not have received an answer to your question, but trust that something was indeed given to you by those spirits, and that answers will come in time. The sharing was there, whether visible or not, and answers will come.

CHAPTER 7

HEEDING THE CALL

It's important to learn how to see with the eyes closed.
LAME DEER, LAKOTA MEDICINE MAN

In retrospect, riding my motorcycle quickly up the steep ramp of the rented U-Haul truck had not been a good idea.

At the top of the ascent, the bike hit a bump in the ramp and crashed down with the momentum that had been carrying it into the truck. I, on the other hand, went flying five feet in the air before smashing, no helmet, onto the concrete driveway. I could not sit up or get up, and night was falling. Fortunately, a neighbor had seen what happened and called an ambulance. She was also a nurse, and came rushing to my side, encouraging me to lie still and not try to get up. Still I tried, but could not put any weight on my legs. Pain shot through me like a lightning strike. I tried wiggling my hands and feet, anxious that I might have broken my spine, but they were OK. Hallelujah!—but still, I couldn't move.

Drawing from years of psychedelic shamanic work, I reminded myself that I was more than my body. Suddenly, I was floating ten feet in the air, having an out-of-body experience, looking down at my body lying in pain in the street.

"This is just another bardo state," I heard an inner voice say with startling clarity—"bardo" referred to a Tibetan Buddhist term for a state of existence intermediate between two lives on Earth. *"You are still*

and always in the infinite space of Now. The story you tell yourself will create your experience."

Taking that in, I reflected, *What story do I want to tell myself about what is happening right now?* The answer came quickly. *I want healing to start right now!* Then came guidance.

"Forgive yourself for what you did. Breathe in peace, breathe in love—send it into the pain. See healing happening. Give thanks that you are alive. This could have taken you out. Let go of judgment. Release. Visualize healing light and love flowing to your injured bones and body."

Soon, an ambulance arrived, its siren howling in the dark night, and I was placed on a stretcher and whisked to the nearest emergency room. Hooked up to an IV drip, morphine and then Dilaudid streamed into my veins to control the pain. However, it did not help, nor did it dull the sound of the busy Friday night, accident-filled waiting room. It was hard to breathe.

Eventually, I was taken for tests to ascertain the extent of my injuries. By the grace of God and my Angels of Protection, I thankfully had no head injury or concussion, and no spinal injury. I had fractured a rib and bruised my leg, hip, and shoulder. The doctors informed me that it would take eight weeks to heal. I decided to use the whole situation as an opportunity to work my "Wake Up, Wise Up, Live Love Now" mantra as a guiding focus during the healing process. I also reflected on the teachings this situation was trying to bring to my awareness. The message echoed what I had learned during my mountain climbing days as a younger man: "Do not let desire overrule your judgment!" It was time to take this lesson to a deeper level of integration.

I felt immense gratitude for how I had been protected from more severe injuries. I could have been paralyzed, brain damaged, or even killed. I spent a lot of time expressing gratitude and reflecting on how my years of psychedelic shamanic practice had served me well in responding to the accident I had caused myself.

"Psychedelic shamanism" refers to the usage of time-tested shamanic practices to activate connection, attunement, and communion with the underlying reality of infinite, unconditional cosmic love-light that is the essence of our being. It involves living from that essence in, with, and through all our relationships, as Wisdom Warriors.

Psychedelic shamanism nurtures the growth of Wisdom Warriors. From early on in the course of my sixty years of using psychedelics in a ceremonial way, I knew it was a sacred endeavor to be entered in to with great respect. Sure, it can be fun to "Turn on, tune in, drop out," as popularized by Timothy Leary in 1966, but I knew from my father's death when I was young just how precarious life is. I had already experienced enough "dropping out" during the dark years of my acting out delinquent behavior. The Indigenous emphasis on being in humble and respectful right relationship with psychedelic plants has been a guiding light that has served me well.

Along with vision questing, working with plant medicine became my primary methods for inducing major consciousness shifts moving from a wounded, fearful, ego-based identity predicated on an illusory perception of separation to an attuned alignment with the infinite field of love-light in which all of creation is interwoven. Both experiences provide powerful insights to previously unconscious obstacles in the psyche that reduce or prevent living in awareness of love's presence.

To be clear, you can reach states of psychedelic consciousness without taking a psychoactive substance. As a reminder, when I refer to the term "psychedelic," I am referring to an expanded state of consciousness. Being a hard nut to crack, I needed the boundary dissolving capacity of psychedelics to open me up, but not everyone needs to go this route. Meditation, yoga, shamanic practices of prayer, fasting, drumming, ecstatic dance and movement, pranayama breathing practices, chanting, singing, listening to uplifting music, T'ai Chi and Qigong, playing musical instruments, rock climbing, running, surfing, paddleboarding, biking, kayaking, hiking, mountaineering, and scuba diving—each of these, when done with intention and focused mindfulness, can raise consciousness to the interwoven nature of reality and to our true nature: infinite, unconditional light and love, that is, psychedelic consciousness.

While the usage of psychedelic plants has been and continues to be instrumental in my personal growth, it is important to note that it can be contraindicated in certain situations. If you have high blood pressure, a history of seizures or heart problems, are taking mood altering antianxiety medications, or suffer from a psychiatric disorder, it is advisable to avoid the use of psychedelic substances.

Psychoactive substances are now being used legally, safely, and productively in the medical field by an increasing number of health professionals to effectively treat depression and PTSD. This progress is due in part to the success of Michael Pollan's bestselling book *How to Change Your Mind: What the New Science of Psychedelics Teaches Us About Consciousness, Dying, Addiction, Depression, and Transcendence.* I had the opportunity to be interviewed by Michael as part of his research for the book; you can listen to our subsequent conversation at this link audio.innertraditions.com/psychedelicshaman.

If your primary motivation for using psychedelics is therapeutic, the modern clinical approach, which is gaining popularity, may be suitable for you. On the other hand, if you feel called to explore psychedelic work or engage in a vision quest for psycho-spiritual healing and exploration, the remainder of this book follows more closely that modality, where I share insights gained from Indigenous healers, elders, and medicine people who practice shamanic traditions. These teachings encompass beliefs, values, and behaviors that can guide you in establishing a right relationship with yourself, others, nature, and life itself. Following this model, I have witnessed participants experience relief from existential angst and gain guidance on how to live as a Wisdom Warrior in harmonious alignment with the world around them.

High dosage psychedelics can transport you to an expanded reality where there is no separation between people, animals, plants, the Earth, and the cosmos. This heightened awareness often leads to kinder, more caring, and compassionate behavior toward oneself, Mother Earth, and all beings. However, this stance clashes with political and social institutions rooted in racist white supremacy and economic systems that prioritize financial and material gain over the well-being of people and nature. These systems rely on us remaining oblivious to the interconnectedness of people and places, allowing us to support policies that dump toxic waste near impoverished neighborhoods where People of Color struggle to live, or in remote areas like deserted islands, the ocean, or deep underground. These places and people are perceived as separate, distant, and irrelevant. But in reality they are not separate, nor is anyone or any place.

In mainstream society, psychedelics have instilled fear because those in power understand that these substances dismantle social conditioning, prompting individuals to question the values, norms, beliefs, and behaviors upon which our lives are built. This fear was the driving force behind political pressure to criminalize psychedelics in the 1960s, despite the positive health benefits being reported by researchers in the United States and Europe. The power holders do not want the general population to challenge the Western way of life, which privileges the few at the expense of the majority and the natural cycles we depend on for our existence.

Conversely, in Indigenous cultures, psychoactive plants are revered and used in socially integrative ways, within the context of ceremonies guided by elders and shamans who have undergone extensive initiatory training. Becoming a shaman is not achieved through a brief workshop; it requires a lifetime of experience and wisdom. Indigenous medicine people understand the significance of factors such as set and setting, as well as the importance of screening and preparation before participating in plant ceremonies. Their cultural practices ensure that the outcomes are socially beneficial rather than disruptive. Ironically, the cultures of Western modernity do sanction certain psychoactive plants that benefit economic goals: coffee, tobacco, and sugar to name a few, all of which provide extra energy for people to work longer hours at jobs that more often than not do little to feed their souls. Alcohol, another culturally sanctioned mind altering substance, can have serious health consequences for individuals and society, and yet it is legal. It is also a central nervous system depressant that dulls consciousness.

With that in mind, it is not surprising to see which psychoactive substances are given legal status and are incessantly promoted through advertising. Why? Because it is easier to control people who are dependent and drugged out than those who are awake, aware, and paying attention. It is therefore essential to understand and dismantle the perceptual and cognitive illusions that create a false reality of separation, and instead to Wake Up to an understanding of the true interconnectedness of reality.

Whatever modality you choose to open your consciousness to an expanded state, be it sacred plant use, vision questing, or some other methodology or practice, you will benefit most by approaching it with respect and humility. Additionally, it is crucial to recognize the importance of integration work that will emerge from what you experience, for you will be given homework.

To increase the chances of having a safe and fruitful experience, especially if you are working with psychedelics, it is vital to make sure the following steps are addressed:

1. Mental Preparation
2. Physical Preparation
3. Clear Intention
4. Safe Set and Setting
5. Support during the Experience
6. Integration Tools

MENTAL PREPARATION

It is a good idea to allow at least a week to focus on preparing yourself. This gives your unconscious mind time to arrange and be ready for what the medicine will offer, tuning your psychospiritual, physical, and biochemical aspects to be in the best state to receive and engage with the medicine in a positive and productive manner. Preparation also demonstrates commitment and respect for the intelligence of the plant, which helps open the doorway to the wisdom of truth and the truth of wisdom. This allows for the fullest blossoming of insights, healing, and wisdom teachings for your greatest good.

Indigenous people approach spiritual plant work and vision questing with great respect and reverence. Warren L. d'Azevedo, author of *Straight with the Medicine*, shares Indigenous perspectives on these dynamics.

> Medicine is like electricity. It can run through you and bring about positive changes. Approach it with a purpose [. . .] to become a better person, to live a more authentic and fulfilling life. Once you take it, it starts working on you, uncovering the truth. You can't deceive it. You must face the truth [. . .] it makes you reflect on everything and shows you the path you need to take. It keeps pushing you in the right direction.

The experience of deep communion with nature opens access to a living, animated intelligence while also creating a gateway to the unconscious and higher transpersonal, transdimensional levels of consciousness. The insights that emerge from this experience can come from any of these realms or a combination of them.

Ingesting a psychoactive plant initiates a dialogue between your awareness and the elements that enter your consciousness, which can dissolve ego-based defenses and provide insight to previously hidden aspects. This insight can help release energy blockages and constrictions resulting from childhood wounds, leading to the establishment of new and empowering life patterns that promote health, happiness, meaning, and fulfillment.

It can also be helpful to pay close attention to your dreams in the week prior to taking the medicine. Write them down in a journal and focus on the aspects of the dream that elicit your strongest emotional response. These dreams can provide valuable insights into what lies beneath the surface of your conscious awareness, giving you a heads-up on what might arise during your journey.

PHYSICAL PREPARATION

Another crucial aspect of preparation is what I refer to as "strengthening the container" work, which is essential for effectively managing and utilizing the heightened energy that will flow through your system during the psychedelic experience. Practicing yoga, stretching, meditation, heart-centered prayers, loving-kindness practices, T'ai Chi and Qigong, breathing exercises, mindful and grounding activities all cultivate qualities that will aid you during the journey. These physical practices strengthen your mind's ability to witness and concentrate, enabling you to engage more fruitfully with your experiences.

It is advisable to abstain from sexual activity for five days prior to the journey, in order to allow your psychic energy to build. Refraining from sexual activity demonstrates respect for the spirit of the medicine.

It is also beneficial to limit media inputs and similar stimuli on the day of the session, and for as many days before as you find suitable.

Diet

When you ingest the medicine, you open yourself up to receiving what the plant and tree spirits have to offer. It's important to create a welcoming and nurturing "inner home" for them, allowing them to freely work their magic. Regardless of the substance you choose, it's a good idea to simplify your diet for at least a week beforehand, focusing on wholesome, natural, plant-based foods. Avoid drugs, sugar, alcohol, dairy, salt, caffeine, and fermented foods. I strongly suggest avoiding meat altogether.

For ayahuasca usage, a stringent diet is required for the week leading up to the session. Ayahuasca prefers a bland, primarily vegetarian cuisine to kickstart the cleansing process. For five to seven days prior to the session, eliminate foods that are aged or fermented to enhance flavor (blue cheese, Roquefort, Parmesan, Romano, cheddar, smoked brie, cream, yogurt, miso, or pickles), avocados, fried or processed foods, figs, raisins, ginseng, protein extracts (including liquid and powdered dietary supplements), dietary supplements containing yeast (baking yeast is safe), chocolate, soy sauce, snails, green or chili peppers, spices, garlic, citrus, stimulants such as coffee, and supplements and protein drinks containing the amino acid tyramine.

The aforementioned foods contain high quantities of the amino acid L-Tyrosine, which produces the contraindicated chemical tyramine in the body, potentially causing a dangerous reaction. This substance can remain in the body for up to three days.

A diet consisting of rice, whole grains, fresh fruit, and simply cooked vegetables without spices is ideal. Additionally, sesame seeds, tahini, almonds, whole grain breads, popcorn, cereals, fruits (excluding citrus), salt free soup, carrot juice, and salads with light dressings using canola oil instead of olive oil are recommended.

The dietary restrictions serve as a test, demonstrating to ayahuasca your willingness to let go of something significant and step out of your ego's comfort zone in pursuit of your intentions.

This journey is not just about taking; it's about giving as well. From an Indigenous perspective, it's crucial to remember that you are not merely dealing with a physical object or a pharmaceutical substance. You are engaging with the spirit of the plant, a living conscious entity that listens to your words and observes your actions, taking note of how you treat it. When the plant spirit feels respected, appreciated, honored, and cared for, it is more likely to share its powerful medicine with you—as with human relationships, you reciprocate when you feel respected and cared for. It's all about fostering a meaningful relationship.

Medications

If you are taking any medications, it is important to consult with the ceremonial leader, as well as your doctor, to determine if there are potential contraindications with the specific plant you plan to ingest. Some medications may need to be discontinued prior to taking the psychedelic substance in order to ensure safety, as mixing certain substances can be life threatening. It is crucial to avoid tranquilizers, antibiotics, amphetamine-type drugs or medications (including ephedrine, procaine preparations, epinephrine, methyldopa, and phenylpropanolamine found in over-the-counter cold preparations).

Additionally, it is necessary to eliminate all narcotics, barbiturates, antihistamines, and analgesics from your system, as well as any ephedrine contained in herbal stimulants, cold remedies, or Chinese herbal remedies.

Please note: It is always important to consult with a medical professional or qualified ceremonial leader for personalized advice regarding medication interactions and safety guidelines.

CLEAR INTENTION

Your part in this dialogue begins with your intention. What are you seeking? Why do you seek it? If you obtain what you're seeking, how will you utilize it? It's important to recognize that this process may not be easy, and could even necessitate significant changes in your life. Are you seeking healing, spiritual communion, creative expression, or raising your consciousness? What are you willing to contribute in relation to your quest?

Answering these questions before embarking on the journey helps to clarify your intention, which will guide you throughout the experience and the integration process, once the effects of the medicine have subsided.

SAFE SET AND SETTING

It is vitally important to make sure the setting of your journey provides physical safety and protection from outside forces and that you feel safe and secure in its location. You want to be able to relax and surrender into your experience not worrying about your safety. It is also crucial to make a wise choice when selecting the leader of the ceremony who will guide you to other dimensions and realms of reality for he or she provides a "set," a framework of values and intentionality that will have an impact on your experience. Be clear about your own set, your personal intentions, and then carefully assess the integrity, honesty, and competence of the facilitator. They will be assisting you in navigating the various challenges and experiences that may arise, much like a labor coach helps with childbirth. It is important that they understand and support your intentions for the journey. To find the right guide or guides for your journey, I recommend the following three-step process:

Step 1: Ask Spirit to guide you to someone who will support your greatest good.

Step 2: Do your research. If you don't know of anyone personally, go online and search for psychedelic journey guides. Do diligent research, paying attention to what calls your interests and values. Check out their references. Look for people with a history of doing this work, not just what my daughters refer to as "pop-up shamans."

Step 3: Engage in internal research. Once you have identified a potential guide, go inward to access the deep wisdom within you—the place that knows what you may not consciously know—your higher self. Consult your spiritual helpers and guides. Then, with receptivity and humility, listen with the fullness of your multidimensional being, not just with your ears. Observe signals that arise—bodily sensations, intuition, dreams, serendipitous events, and synchronicities. When you receive a green light, engage in a conversation with the person, asking any questions that come to mind. Observe how they respond and how you respond to their answers.

By following these steps, you can find a guide who is aligned with your intentions and can provide the support and guidance needed for a transformative and safe psychedelic journey.

INTEGRATION TOOLS

More often than not your journey experience will give you homework assignments. You will have insights, understandings, feedback, and realizations about changes you need to make in your life if you want to grow in a healthy way. This speaks to the process of integrating what you have learned into the challenges of daily life. This starts with your intention to do so. When the assignments are honored you will receive more.

Start your day with empowering your intention to use what you have been given in all your interactions and relationships. Enter into a meditative state and recite to yourself what you want to do and see yourself doing so in your imagination with clear visualization. Finish your day with a review of how you did: where you succeeded and where you didn't. Congratulate yourself for the successes and learn from what made you drop the ball. No judgment. Instead compassion and forgiveness for your humanity, and going deeper to explore root causes of reactive behavior. Practice in your imagination how to meet the same stimuli in a more skillful manner incorporating the wisdom teachings from your altered state journey. Turn what are initially perceived as problems into opportunities to work your integration process, remembering your intention, and use each day to progress in your efforts.

Remember that today is the only day you ever have so use it wisely to enrich your life and the life around you.

Trust your inner wisdom guidance. Trust Spirit.

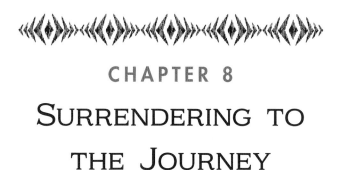

CHAPTER 8

SURRENDERING TO
THE JOURNEY

Let go release, whatever needs to go. Open and receive,
love's healing flow.

W hat should I do while on the journey? What will it be like? What will happen to me?" These are frequently asked questions as questers prepare to journey. Eminent Czechoslovakian LSD researcher Stanislav Grof believes the psychedelic experience has four stages:

STAGE I
Physical and Somatic Effects

The medicine is starting to take effect and the doorway is opening. There may be some initial disorientation. This is the time to take deep breaths, relax, surrender, and let go. Allow yourself to be carried downstream, like a leaf on a river. Bring forth your observing witness and be fully present to absorb it all. This is why you came. The gates are opening. Hunt what you seek like a jaguar stalking its prey.

STAGE 2
Material from the Personal Unconscious, the Collective Unconscious, or the Transpersonal Higher Consciousness Begins to Pour through the Container of Your Mind

You are now on the hero's path. Remain open to it all. It is likely that previously repressed material will emerge from the unconscious. This is good, because now you can work consciously with what, in your ordinary everyday state, was not available. The power of unconscious energies to trigger troubling reactive behaviors can and frequently does diminish when brought to the light of conscious awareness.

STAGE 3
Ego Loss

This can occur through feelings and or visions of death and dying, destruction, dismemberment. Remember, for the new to come through there first has to be a death/letting go of the old. Ego-based identity, with its need to control, has to be released in order to connect, attune, and commune with the higher numinous presence of Spirit underlying all manifestation. Before spring, fall arrives, followed by the dark of winter. After the work of winter has been completed, then—and only then—come the blessings of the fourth stage.

STAGE 4
Rebirth

Facing the "hell" realms can bring you through to the "heavenly" realms of oneness, union, ecstasy, bliss, and connection with the Divine. In these states, you receive wisdom guidance for healing, transformation, empowerment, and soul growth.

In working with sacred plants, or any aspect of nature for that matter— mountains, lakes, rivers, streams, meadows, trees, animals, birds, insects, wind, sky, sun, moon, stars, rocks, the Earth herself—it is critical to remember that you are not just interacting with a physical entity. Each and every entity has consciousness, a spirit. The experience is a two-way exchange.

Just as humans are more than bodies and ego identities, so too is a psychedelic plant—it's not just a physical substance. The plant has consciousness, non-human intelligence, and its essence is Spirit, just as your essence is Spirit. Recognize that a previously living conscious being is giving its life to help you with your life. In this light, it is important that the spirit of the medicine be respected, thanked, and appreciated.

You might seek a numinous vision, a connection with ancestors, healing of some sort, or a behavioral change of an unhealthy life pattern. You might get what you seek or you might not, but the medicine is always working within you. The spirit wisdom of the plant might deem it more important for you to receive something other than a blissful experience or what you initially sought. You might experience a dark night of the soul, showing how you have burdened your life with toxic negative beliefs about yourself, thoughtforms of limitation, shame, guilt, or self-pity.

If you seek healing, if you seek transformation, remember that you only have the power to change what you face and accept. You can't change any aspect of unhealthy or unskillful behavioral patterns unless you acknowledge them as part of your psychological makeup. These thoughts and patterns are not who you are—if you want to break free from them and replace them with healthier patterns, you must confront the truth of what is.

Doing shadow work is like descending to the basement of an old house to uncover the hidden termite rot that may be ingrained in the foundation. You must bring the rot of what mystic teacher Gurdjieff referred to as a personal "ship of fools"—ego vanity, selfishness, meanness, narcissism, potential for violence, inflated sense of self-importance and entitlement—to the light of conscious awareness. It is crucial to recognize that what we avoid confronting ultimately exerts control over us. If we seek spiritual wholeness, we must establish a sacred relationship with all aspects of our being and all facets of reality during our human existence.

Each of us develops a sense of ego identity as we grow. Ego itself is not inherently negative; it serves practical purposes such as ensuring our safety when crossing the street or maintaining oral hygiene. However, problems arise when we mistakenly equate our entire being with our ego and the narratives it constructs. This disconnects us from our soul, our deeper essence of who we truly are. Skillful use of psychedelics can shed light on the dynamics of ego identity.

Entering a powerful psychedelically altered state can dissolve the cognitive-linguistic structures that create and uphold our ego-based identity. This may give rise to a sensation of "losing one's mind," which can trigger fear and anxiety. To counteract this fear, it is important to remember that the mind you are temporarily releasing is the one unconsciously conditioned by your upbringing and culture. Temporary release can actually be a positive experience, as it offers an opportunity to transcend that conditioning. It allows you to expand your consciousness and connect with the deeper truth of your existence—a divine spark, intricately connected to the universe and its infinite wellspring of creative wisdom potential.

ON THE DAY OF YOUR JOURNEY

On the day of your journey, I recommend a twenty-four-hour water or juice fast, unless you have a medical condition that would prohibit it. Fasting helps purge toxins and strengthens your intentionality, so that you can enter into the sacred with receptivity, respect, and humility, all of which can help promote a positive experience. Remember to drink plenty of water or natural fruit or vegetable juices to stay hydrated.

Fear and Anxiety

When it's time for your journey to altered states, give yourself permission to experience fear and anxiety. This is natural. You are entering the unknown, and you are not in control of what will happen. Even after all my years of this work, I still feel anxiety rise up in me at times. Why? Because my ego-self clings to its creature comforts, its false sense of control, and its familiarity with predictable experiences based on habitual routines. But these habitual activities and thought patterns, referred to by neuroscientists as the default mode function of the brain, can lock you into an unhealthy cycle of habituation and stagnation. Accepting the presence of anxiety and fear is a necessary step when preparing for a psychedelic journey because the ego knows it will be pushed out of its comfort zone.

When the default mode goes offline, it opens up connections to previously constricted awareness channels, bringing new ways of seeing, being, and relating to yourself and others that can nourish the soul. When our souls are nourished, our light shines brighter, and we become healthier, happier, and more attuned to the flow of creative intelligence in the universe.

Remember Your Intention

Before ingesting the plant medicine, take a few moments to recall your intention. Breathe deeply, allowing your breath to reach your heart chakra. Visualize a beam of energy extending from your heart to the spirit of the plant. Express gratitude for its existence and life. Explain to the plant why you are seeking its guidance and healing, and what you are willing to offer in return. Have faith that the spirit of the plant is attentive, as we are interconnected with all of creation at the profoundest level. Express your gratitude and invoke the plant's assistance in your journey.

Surrender and Listen

Once you have ingested the medicine, doors open and you are not in charge or control of what comes through those doors.

> *Whatever shows up in your journey is not by accident. Deeper wisdom is trying to bring something into your consciousness for you to see.*

During the experience, you may or may not enter a visionary state. Regardless, the medicine is working to clear and heal spiritual, mental, emotional, and physical wounds and blockages. This often begins with bodily sensations, frequently in the abdominal area.

Take deep breaths, relax your body, and allow the medicine to circulate freely. Be receptive, humble, and grateful. Remember to surrender— and surrender to remember. If you judge or resist what is being offered, tension and anxiety may increase. Instead, visualize healing love-light flowing to you with each breath, using your out breath to release tension and fear. If you encounter a fearful presence, stand your ground and inquire, "What are you here to teach me? What are you here to show me that I need to confront?"

Ask yourself, "How can I create a response to what I am experiencing (fear or anxiety) that grows me in a direction I want to grow and is for my greatest good?"

Let go of resisting what you are experiencing, of wanting it to be different than what it is. Whatever shows up in your journey is not by accident. Deeper wisdom is trying to bring something to your consciousness to see, explore, work with, confront, make peace with, and/or transform. The illuminating light of psychedelic awareness brings insight to destructive patterns and the price you pay through their activity. Stay present with your witness function. See, learn, and absorb all you can. Wake Up to the truth.

Skillfully working with psychedelic challenges—facing fears and shadow material—helps to clear the path, opening access to the numinous. This, in turn, brings the revelation that you are much more than you think you are. This expanded understanding of identity reduces anxiety and fear about mortality, and provides a broader perspective to embrace the cyclic ups and downs of daily life, strengthening resilience in the face of challenges and uncertainties.

While we do not have control over what happens in the world, we can learn to use the instrumentality of our minds to connect, attune, and commune with the creating wisdom power of the universe, drawing on its infinite resources to make conscious choices about we want to experience in the moment. That choice is something we do have control over—if we take responsibility for the state of our minds, using them to Wake Up, Wise Up, and Live Love Now. We truly have the ability to create a peaceful, just, healthy, happy, and harmonious Win-Win World for All. Responsible engagement with psychedelic shamanism can open awareness to our individual and collective highest potentials, enabling us to manifest this potential as Wisdom Warriors.

Modern science tells us that, through the process of neuroplasticity, the wisdom in our body knows how to create new brain cells with the right stimulation, which any kind of new learning can provide. Research on the effects of psychedelic experience on the brain shows that it opens new channels of connection and stimulates neuroplasticity. Psychedelic shamanic practices enable actual altering of the structure of the physical brain by creating sustained shifts in our practices of thought and behavior. But it takes consistency of practice to shapeshift a temporary state to an altered trait. Psychedelic shamanism, as I have defined it, opens the awareness channel to our higher potentials, as individuals and as a collective, so we can show up as Wisdom Warriors and do our part, bringing the kind of world we envision to physical existence.

FINDING YOUR MIND

Throughout your journey, utilize everything that emerges on the shores of your consciousness. Waste nothing. Trust the wisdom of whatever presents itself. If fear arises, embrace it, bring it into the light, and confront it directly. Ask what you can learn from the things that frighten you. Treat them as allies that aid your personal growth by understanding their origins, what sustains them, and how they function. Your journey will assign you tasks, so be sure to honor them as an essential part of integration—the actual work of incorporating what you have learned into your everyday existence.

CHAPTER 9

Integration

It is easy to open your mouth
to take in a psychoactive substance.
It is much more challenging to
bring its teachings into your daily life.

Integration can be both the most challenging and the most important aspect of psychedelic shamanism. Engaging in quests and sacred plant work can provide valuable insights with the potential to profoundly transform your life. However, it is crucial to honor and integrate these insights into your ongoing life—the real value of the experience lies in what you do with it once you return. It is important to allow yourself time to initiate the process of integration. Take it slowly as you reenter your regular life.

During the crucial first days after your journey, stay open to new insights revealing themselves, bringing more clarity and understanding of what you experienced. It is helpful to record in a journal a full account of what you went through, what you saw and what you learned, along with assignments or homework the medicine gave you. Make drawings or paintings of the images or visions, allowing their energy to emerge and express themselves in different ways. Make use of musical instruments—drums, rattles, guitars, sound bowls, or whatever you have around—to help with your reflections. Open to new creativity coming through you. Pay attention to your dreams—you have opened doorways to both higher and lower consciousness, so track what comes through this opening.

Be kind and gentle to yourself and others. Your perception and cognitive sense making functions have shifted, as your assemblage point has moved. You now experience yourself, reality, and your relationships from a different perspective. Daily life incidents will test your commitment to integration and your willingness to act upon and honor the assignments that arise. These assignments may involve healing relationship wounds, initiating projects you've been avoiding out of fear, breaking unhealthy patterns, or making positive changes in your diet, exercise, or posture.

As you navigate the integration process, remember to connect with your inner child, who may feel fearful amid the changes. Keep your heart open, even in challenging situations that push your buttons. It can be helpful to frame these situations as tests of your spiritual growth, opportunities to integrate and ground what you have learned. When faced with difficulties, you have the chance to practice and strengthen your spiritual understanding. Share the love in your heart with yourself and others on a daily basis. Consider incorporating chants and mantras (ch. 13) into your practice.

New insights, visions, information, inspiration, healing, and empowerment require regular nourishment in order to flourish and reach their full potential. Without consistent attention and care, the gifts obtained from your journey may gradually fade or lose their impact.

By diligently doing your homework, you open yourself up to more gifts of insight, understanding, and personal power. However, if you neglect to honor and integrate what you have received, your energy and creativity may become stagnant and blocked.

To keep your energy flowing and gratitude alive, it is essential to express appreciation to the spirit of the plants. Here are some ways to show gratitude and give back:

◄ Engage in efforts that address environmental, social, and cultural challenges our world faces. Stand against assaults on the Earth, its oceans, Indigenous people, People of Color, minorities, and the natural cycles of life. Support initiatives for the protection of endangered ecosystems, forests, oceans, plants, animals, and their habitats. Advocate for politicians and policies that combat global warming. Work toward peace, social and economic justice, and innovative ways to sustain and rejuvenate biodiversity on Earth.

◀ Offer prayers for the lives and families of the plant people, as they too face threats and challenges. Extend your thoughts and intentions to their well-being.

◀ Minimize your impact on the Earth and her life support systems by choosing sustainably made, reusable products. Extend gratitude and acknowledgment to everyone involved in the creation, production, and delivery of the items you use.

By actively showing appreciation and taking meaningful action, you contribute to the well-being of the natural world and maintain a harmonious relationship with the gifts you have received.

Time and again, I have been presented with testing opportunities to apply the lessons I've learned from psychedelic journeys. Unplanned events occur, attempting to activate old patterns of reactivity to see whether I will allow them to control me or instead choose to apply the wisdom gained from my journeys. You can expect to experience this same process in your life.

Indigenous elders often refer to these tests as the work of the trickster. The trickster is an archetype that appears in cultures across human history, taking on various forms, such as the clown, jester, joker, buffoon, or holy fool. Tricksters often deceive themselves, and may even find themselves in dangerous situations due to their foolishness. However, they always manage to come back to life. Despite their flaws, they carry profound teachings and insights. By reflecting our own foolishness and toxic reactive patterns, they challenge our self-importance and empower us to live a more consciously chosen life.

In the Northwestern Indigenous traditions of North America (Turtle Island), the trickster figure manifests as Raven. In the Great Lakes region, it is the Hare. And for the Indigenous people of California, it is the Coyote or Coyote Man.

Coyote tales are shared as teaching stories in Indigenous communities, particularly for young individuals. Coyote's mischief serves as a wake-up call, helping people recognize and confront the ego's hubris, entitlement, and inflated sense of superiority. It prompts us to acknowledge our personal weaknesses and the forces that hinder the expansion of our consciousness.

As you embark on your Heart Path to Completion, you learn to nourish your soul rather than feed your ego. You grow into a Wisdom Warrior, doing your best and fully enjoying each moment with the awareness that every action could be your last.

I was given a challenging assignment during a psychedelic shamanic mushroom journey, which brought about numerous tests in the form of coyote-like situations. The assignment was clear: "Carry your heart through the world like a life-giving sun, shining brightly upon everyone you encounter."

Shortly after, I received the same message in a dream during a vision quest, but with more specific instructions: "Keep your heart open and extend unconditional love and light to each person you meet every day, or anyone who comes to your awareness."

It didn't take long for the first test to appear.

I encountered difficulty at my local bank when the teller at the outside window refused to accept the checks I was trying to deposit. I was in a rush to get to an appointment at my office, and frustration and anger clouded my emotions as I went inside and approached the teller. Luckily, I realized the negative energy I was projecting, as if punishing her for my own inconvenience. In that moment, I awakened from my reactivity and noticed the contradiction between my intention to honor my assignment and my actions toward the innocent bank clerk.

Wake Up, tomás! This is your opportunity to let go of your ego attachments and sense of entitlement, and return to your original intention. Clean up your act, release the negative energy, open your heart again, forgive yourself, and get back on track. Send sweet love and light energy to this person, who is just trying to do their job!

It's not a coincidence that the homework given during a spiritual medicine journey gets challenged when you try to integrate and apply it. These challenges are opportunities for you to make a conscious decision. Ask yourself: "Am I going to allow myself to get caught up in this reactive pattern, disregarding my intention? Or am I going to break this habit and realign myself to honor my assignment?"

Without facing these tests, there will be little empowerment or growth. Each time we consciously and skillfully work with what is presented to us, we gain strength and momentum in integrating the teachings from our journey into our daily life.

Here's another example:

During an ayahuasca experience, a song and its lyrics came to me, along with a message to set them to music. That was the easy part. I came home, picked up my guitar, and strummed the chords that complemented the words effortlessly. The song, titled *Thank You Plant People*, flowed smoothly as I sang it to myself, relishing in its harmonious sound. This heartfelt composition served as a thanks-giving ode to the precious offerings bestowed by the sacred teachers—the plants, true elders of Mother Earth, who have graced her presence long before our arrival. You can listen to *Thank You Plant People* at audio.innertraditions.com/psychedelicshaman.

The tests kept coming. On a subsequent ayahuasca journey one month later, the medicine told me to sing the song in public. This really pushed my buttons—I was extremely self-conscious about singing in front of others. I frequently went off tune and my guitar skills were rudimentary. Suffice it to say, this assignment was far beyond my ego's comfort zone.

Resistance was immediate. *No, I don't have to do this. I can just enjoy the song myself. I don't have to embarrass myself in public and set myself up for ridicule!*

But then I remembered my intention in doing the journey. I gave myself permission to feel anxious, fearful, and vulnerable, but didn't let those feelings stop me from doing what I'd signed up to do: honor my homework assignments and bring them into my daily life.

Shortly thereafter, I gathered my courage and tentatively sang the song to a few close friends, accompanied by the guitar chords I had put together. The universe didn't end, and I survived. People actually said they liked it, and for once my voice had been in tune. Praise be, a miracle!

The next test came after I received fourteen additional songs, which I also put to guitar accompaniment. *"Make a CD recording of the songs."* This was too much. I had no clue how to make a CD, let alone raise the funds to do so. A ton of fear-based negativity messages burst forth, testing my willingness to go forward. *Who do you think you are? You're not a talented singer, musician, or performer. You're just a narcissistic fool trying to get attention. Don't be an idiot. Get a life!*

From deep within, another voice emerged to combat the first one: *"Live in integrity and honor the spirit of Mother Ayahuasca by acting on what you have been tasked to do. It is part of your spiritual curriculum. Are you going to do your homework only when it's in your comfort zone? Are you going to give your power away to fear? Or will you go ahead with what you are tasked to do, with faith and trust that it will all work out for the fullest blossoming and the greatest good?"*

In other words—do you choose love, or do you give your power to fear?

I chose love. I gave myself permission to experience anxiety and fear, but went ahead anyway. I discovered a producer who could help me make the CD, and somehow the funds showed up to make it happen.

After several months of working together, we had a CD of all the songs, titled *Jumping into the Real*, a name inspired by the photo we'd chosen for the CD cover, of my grandsons and me jumping off a cliff in Hawaii. The theme and storyline of the songs start with fear and depression, move through loss and grief, and eventually arrive in joyful union with spirit. I felt a sense of accomplishment in completing this challenging homework assignment. However, it didn't take long for another test of my spiritual growth to present itself, bringing an entirely different challenge: the coyote at work.

Returning home from a wonderful solo birthday retreat, I was greeted by the tenant of our downstairs rental unit with some very foul news, quite literally. Our sewage pipes had broken, and raw sewage was pouring into our yard. The cost of getting it fixed, removing the waste, and cleaning the soil amounted to twenty-two thousand dollars!

I snapped. That was the final straw—this house had already cost me over one hundred thousand dollars in repairs over the past ten years, depleting most of the inheritance my mother left me when she passed.

I stormed into the house, yelling to Andrea, "We are putting this fucking house up for sale today!" I immediately called a realtor to initiate the process. Now came the daunting task of finding an affordable home in expensive Marin county, where we had lived for almost fifty years. We desperately wanted to remain close to our family, friends, and beloved community. However, with continually rising real estate prices and limited funds, our prospects seemed bleak.

Our house sold quickly, but for less than we had hoped for. Everyone we spoke to—family, friends, real estate agents—expressed the same sentiment: finding the kind of home we wanted in Marin with our financial constraints would be impossible.

Months and months of scanning real estate sites daily on the internet, along with hours spent driving around each day checking out possibilities, created a perfect storm of negativity. Every day of unsuccessful searching meant confronting depression, despair, frustration, fear, doubt, and a gnawing sense of desperation. Finding what we wanted at an affordable price seemed impossible.

However, amid this bleak outlook, I held on to my faith that with Spirit's help anything was possible. I had experienced the power of faith in the past, and knew that, to manifest our desired outcome, I had to keep the light of faith burning despite the strong winds of negativity. I trusted that, by playing my part in the process and with the grace of Spirit, we would be successful in finding what we sought. I also understood that I would face severe tests along the way—and indeed, I did. Daily mantras of faith and trust helped me maintain a positive outlook.

I recognized that the limiting stories created by my ego-based mind did not define me. I am much more than what they say. I am a manifestation of the underlying oneness of infinite, unconditional, cosmic love-light consciousness.

I affirmed my sacredness, worthiness, and luminosity, and acknowledged that I am loved and capable of both giving and receiving love. I reminded myself to Wake Up, Wise Up, and Live Love Now.

After reciting these affirmations, I focused on creating a clear mental image of the house we desired. I visualized every detail of the house, its price, and its location. I imagined us living happily in this home, enjoying the benefits of a smaller, more affordable space with reduced upkeep and maintenance. And in this process, I called upon my trusted spiritual ally, Deer Spirit.

Deer Spirit, known as *Kauyumari* by the Huichol, first appeared to me during my initial vision quest in the Sierra. It arrived just before darkness fell, when my fear of bears was intensifying with the diminishing sunlight. The sight of a physical deer brought me reassurance, reminding me that I was under the guidance of Spirit and would be protected.

Subsequent quests introduced me to other power animals—the bear, the eagle, the butterfly, the rattlesnake. Some appeared in dreams, while others revealed themselves through psychedelic medicine journeys. Each power ally carries a unique energy, so I call upon the one most effective for the specific area in which I need assistance. Hence, I called upon Deer Spirit in its majestic buck form with antlers to aid in opening doorways and overcoming obstacles to finding our new home.

Expressing gratitude for Deer Spirit's presence and support throughout my life, I offered prayers for the well-being and protection of its people. Then, I requested its assistance in activating the cosmic web of infinite mystery, where all things are possible, to help locate the perfect house and guide us to it. Every day, through visualization, I pictured Andrea and me living happily, healthily, and gratefully in our new home.

Maintaining a positive mindset during this visualization practice required facing and dissolving any doubts or negative thoughts that entered my mind. Allowing them to take root would hinder my efforts in finding our ideal house. It was a challenging task, as the facts repeatedly contradicted what I sought to manifest. To uphold a positive energy, I summoned a resilient warrior spirit and affirmed my intentions. Furthermore, I understood the importance of regularly nourishing my Deer Spirit ally with positive energy, fueling its search for our dream home.

After months of futile searching, pressured by the approaching deadline for when we needed to be out of our house, a miracle happened: we found a house Andrea and I both liked, in a great location, at a price we could afford. We made it! It happened!

The image of the house I had created in my mind, fueled by faith and positive energy applied over time, finally resulted in its manifestation in the outer world. Finding the house was a huge affirmation of what I call an inner gardening process, one that requires diligently staying the course with faith and trust while surrendering the ego's timing to divine timing and maintaining a high level of positive energy.

Tests of spiritual assignments given in psychedelic journey work challenge the integration process. They push the buttons of reactivity— and in these situations we have the opportunity to see and confront the stories we tell ourselves from an ego-identity perspective, stories that create suffering. We can choose to unplug from these unconsciously conditioned patterns and stories, and instead create a conscious new story of living based on love rather than fear.

If you follow the guidance of your heart's wisdom on a daily basis, you will nourish your soul and actualize your potential to live as a Psychedelic Shamanic Wisdom Warrior. When you come to the end of your life, you can look back and feel content with how you lived, then peacefully release into the mystery of death, the next adventure in exploring the sacred mystery.

STEP THREE

Live Love Now

*As a Spiritual Warrior channeling the
infinite, unconditional cosmic love-light stardust flowing into
and through us out into the world, in all relationships
working to Heal the Sacred Hoop.*

CHAPTER 10

OPENING TO YOUR PURPOSE

You are not here by accident;
you have purpose in being here.

One of the many meaningful results of a consciousness-expanding experience with sacred plants or vision quest is that of facing your mortality, which can help shed light on what you most value—which therein holds clues to finding your life's purpose, your path of heart. We never know when the next breath might be our last, which compels us to contemplate the meaning and significance of our lives. As humans, we are innate meaning makers, driven by our prefrontal cerebral cortex.

However, mainstream Eurocentric culture often fails to provide necessary support to help individuals embrace their mortality and cultivate a sense of soulful purpose. This deficiency is reflected in rising rates of depression, suicide, violence, obesity, and stress related illnesses. Indigenous cultures, on the other hand, have long recognized the importance of initiatory experiences for young people entering adolescence. These rites of passage guide individuals in discovering meaningful purposes that not only benefit their own lives but also contribute to the well-being of their community.

Initiatory rites across different cultures acknowledge the inevitability of death and the uncertainty surrounding its timing. Confronting the reality of mortality prompts deep reflection on how one is living their life at present. It raises questions about alignment with one's values, authenticity, integrity, and the pursuit of meaning.

On my second year of pilgrimage with the Huichol, in 1982, I had a visionary experience which dramatically illuminated my purpose with great clarity. Led by the shaman, a group of twenty or so Huichols and a handful of gringos traveled three hundred miles from the rancho in Tepic to the sacred high desert land of Wiricuta to hunt for the peyote cactus, which is a sacrament of Huichol spiritual cosmology. Guided by Deer Spirit Kauyumari, I successfully collected an ample supply of peyote for our upcoming all-night ceremony, which would be led by the shaman around the sacred fire, whose spirit is called Tatewari.

Amid my search, I stumbled upon a fist-sized peyote unlike any I had encountered before. It boasted delicate white and pink flower petals, with more buds ready to bloom. Its beauty stood in stark contrast to the barren desert surroundings, leaving me awestruck. In that moment, an innate desire arose to bring this beauty back home with me.

No, you can't do that, my rational mind said. *Possession of peyote by non-Indians is illegal in the United States. You will be arrested at the border. Besides, even if you could take the cactus home, the flower would wilt before you got there.*

Standing there transfixed, a new thought arose. *Maybe I could eat it and take it home inside me!* I didn't know if Huichol protocol allowed for harvesting and eating flowering peyote; the last thing I wanted was to violate a sacred norm that might upset the delicate protocol of the pilgrimage.

So I walked over to one of the Huichol elders who was harvesting plants a few yards away, to ask if it was OK to act on my desire to take the beautifully delicate flower into my body by eating it.

To my delight, the elder gave her blessing, saying it was good medicine to take in, "To sweeten your heart." Little did I know what was to come.

Later that evening, I lay in my sleeping bag around the fire, completely under the effects of the peyote I had consumed.

The flowers of love reside within your heart, bestowed by the wise creative power of the universe.

Suddenly, I felt a pounding in the center of my chest. Immediately, I brought my awareness down to my heart to ensure everything was OK. And then it began.

A vision of the beautiful flower I had eaten appeared in the middle of my heart. *Oh yes, this is wonderful,* I thought. I was so happy to see it. It was beautiful. The flower gently shook from side to side for a moment, and then divided into another flower. *Wow, this is great.*

I watched in fascination, wondering what might come next. To my amazement, the second flower divided into a third flower, and then another, and another, until a burst of flowers filled my heart with joyful ecstasy.

"These are flowers of love," a voice said. *"This is what it's like when your heart is full of love. The blossoming flowers bring joy."*

This was enough for me, but the flowers kept multiplying. There was no more room in my heart to hold them. I watched in complete absorption as the flowers expanded from my heart and began flowing through my body. Soon, my entire being was filled with the exquisite beauty of the flowers. But the flow didn't cease. The flowers continued to pour in.

The voice spoke once again. *"Start sending these love flowers out to the world. Send them to whomever you desire. Infuse the hearts of those you choose with this abundance, so they too can experience the joy of love that you are feeling."*

Every morning after that experience, I've cultivated a connection with this task in my prayers. I recall the profound feeling, and know that I can summon these love flowers from my heart and send them to others whenever I wish. The Huichol people refer to these flowers as *tutus,* and they are always available in infinite supply. Even if you have never been to Wirikuta or experienced peyote, you still possess your own version of these love flowers. The seeds of love flowers reside within your heart, bestowed by the wise creative power of the universe. You can access them whenever you choose to connect and release yourself from the suffocating grip of self-judgment, criticism, and negative comparison to others. Whenever you let go of limited definitions imposed by the ego and awaken to your true nature, these love flowers come forth.

If you pay close attention, you will notice that with each breath you are constantly creating your sense of self and shaping your experience in the present moment. Each breath carries a hidden question we often overlook. "What do you wish to create with this precious gift of life flowing into you? How do you want to utilize it? Will you open your awareness to the presence of love or will you create suffering? The choice is yours."

Being fully present in the moment and consciously making choices may not always be easy. Our spirits reside in a temporary time/space vessel, housing a reptilian brain and monkey mind within an animal body—with its own sometimes conflicting agendas. However, this is the work that fosters growth and enables us to fulfill our shared human purpose—embodying our full humanity and striving to live as agents of conscious evolution. Ultimately, if you and I do not Live Love Now, who will? If we do not act now, then when? The present moment is the only time in which we can create and experience the life and world we desire to live in.

FOUR KEY STEPS

While we all share the overarching assignment of awakening to remember, connect, and live from our true divine love essence, it is important to recognize that each of us also has a unique and specific purpose. If you have already discovered your purpose, that's wonderful—keep pursuing it. If you are still seeking clarity, here are four keys I've gleaned from personal experience and from guiding thousands of individuals through ceremonies and counseling work over the past five decades.

Key 1: Remember that everything starts with intention.
In whatever way works for you, let the universe know that you sincerely want to discover your purpose for this life. Wise counsel in this regard can be found in Matthew 7:7–8 of the King James Bible: "Ask, and it

shall be given you; seek, and ye shall find; knock, and it shall be opened unto you: For every one that asketh receiveth; and he that seeketh findeth; and to him that knocketh it shall be opened."

Following Matthew's advice requires openness, attentiveness, patience, humility, sincerity, and receptivity to whatever comes your way. Psychedelic journeys can indeed open the door to insights and understanding of life purpose. However, the vision quest, or a similar practice, is a time-honored method through which Indigenous youth sought to discover their purpose and gain the power to live it.

This approach is available to anyone, without the need of consuming mind-altering substances. Thus, it provides a model for modern seekers in search of their life purpose. First and foremost, it involves spending time in nature, as Spirit communicates through the expressions found in the natural world for those who learn to listen, observe, and practice patience, faith, and trust. Every time I guide a group of people on a vision quest, a practice I began in 1972, I witness this phenomenon.*

During a wilderness quest, as participants align themselves with the natural rhythms of the sun rising and setting over the course of days and nights, a gradual synchronization takes place. Questers slow down, becoming more perceptive and attuned. They begin to sense the interconnectedness of all beings and witness the ongoing miracle of creation. In today's world, where we spend so much time indoors with various technological devices such as TVs, cell phones, and computers, we often fail to hear nature's call. We are taught to view ourselves as superior to plants, animals, and other natural elements like mountains, clouds, rain, rocks, and wind, perceiving them as separate entities devoid of consciousness, spirit, or life.

Yet, when we listen, observe, and immerse ourselves in nature, a voice emerges that is difficult to discern amid concrete covered cities. Cold, star-filled nights, steamy Amazonian jungles, seemingly barren deserts,

---

*For a more detailed account, I invite you to read my book *Shamanic Wisdom of the Huichol: Medicine Teachings for Modern Times* (published by Destiny Books in 2010), which delves into how I began conducting vision quest retreats through my work with heroin addicts.

lush forests, and open meadows all possess voices and an energy language. Allow me to share a voice I heard during one of my early quest journeys:

Voice of Nature

"Hear me, Two Leggeds, for I speak the truth. You are my children, but so are All Beings. You must relearn to live in respectful harmony with all your relations, or by your own hand, not mine, you will destroy your only home and take many others with you.

"Hear me, Two Leggeds; come out to what you call the wild places and sit with me awhile. I have much to share with you. I can nourish your soul, promoting healing and well-being. I can assist you in remembering your true identity and purpose for being here. However, I need your help. I require your cooperation. Please, for your own sake, heed my call."

Allow the Voice of Nature, both within and without, to guide you in discovering your deeper purpose and the unique gifts you have to offer life.

Key 2: Learn to read the information you are given and respond skillfully.

Imagine being a surfer, sitting on your board in the vast ocean, completely at the mercy of the waves. Focus your attention on the ever-changing conditions rolling in from the horizon. When a wave appears that aligns with your preferences, paddle vigorously to catch it. If your skills are honed, you're rewarded with an exhilarating ride.

The key to catching a wave lies in understanding the information it carries. By reading and interpreting subtle cues and applying your developed skills, you can navigate the wave's energy. A surfer doesn't attempt to control or resist the wave; instead, they learn to flow with it. Similarly, you shouldn't try to control or resist the waves that come to you from the vast ocean of the universe. Rather, learn to read the messages embedded within the waves, enabling you to skillfully navigate the currents of life.

Go beyond mere observation—truly see. Observation is a superficial way of perceiving, whereas seeing involves paying attention to the deeper levels of experience that often go unnoticed. In his book *The Shaman's Body*, Dr. Arnold Mandell refers to this type of seeing as "second attention"—the ability to perceive things that appear on the periphery of awareness, often dismissed as insignificant but which may hold valuable messages if we attune to them. My daughters, who have joined me on many vision quests, refer to it as "seeing with vision quest eyes."

Look within. Close your eyes, and rely on feeling the energy and intuiting its message. Closing off external visual stimuli takes you to a place of introspection, where you can "see" through feeling from your heart and soul. In this state of quieted mind and expanded consciousness, you can access intuitive wisdom and guidance.

Sometimes, inner guidance may urge you toward something that seems daunting or impossible to your rational mind. In such moments, you must decide whether to let fear hold you back or to move forward with faith—even in the face of uncertainty, insecurity, and lack of confidence. The word "impossible" is intriguing; it carries a trickster quality. Place an apostrophe after the letter "i" and a space between "m" and "p," and you get "I'm possible."

You never truly know what's possible unless you show up and give it your all. Only then do you discover your true capabilities. If you surrender your power to fear, you close the doors of possibility, shrink your world, weaken your life force, and never fulfill your purpose.

Successfully navigating the waves of the ocean and the waves of life requires more than physical strength. It demands flexibility and fluidity, in the ability to adapt to rapid changes and uncertainties. It also necessitates inner strength—the strength to let go of ego and surrender to a greater force.

Sufi teacher Hazrat Inayat Khan stated, "Strength is not required to resist the jarring influences of life. There is no wall that can withstand the waves of the ocean. However, a small piece of wood, light and flexible, can rise and fall with the waves, remaining above them, unharmed and safe. The smaller a person's ego becomes, the greater their endurance."

The strength Khan spoke of requires an expansion of consciousness beyond ego identity, coupled with humility and a willingness to surrender to forces greater than oneself.

Remember, you are more than just your body and ego identity. You are part of the creative infinite potential of the universe. Tune in to that source of wisdom, surrender the outcome to its hands, and declare: "I open myself to your presence with gratitude for the abundance of grace in my life. I seek your guidance to fulfill the purpose for which you have granted me life and protected me until this moment. I am determined to honor the path you have laid before me. Thank you for the opportunity to be alive, to open my heart, mind, and soul to fulfill your divine will."

Key 3: Face all aspects of yourself, especially your wounds. See what they and your inner child, who incurred them, need for healing.

It can be excruciatingly difficult to encounter previously repressed feelings or unowned aspects of yourself. It can also be ecstatic and joyful. It can be both. Aligning your intentionality with healing, wholeness, and an expanded awareness of deeper truth enables you to be with and respond to whatever arises in a growth promoting manner. When your starting point is healing and growth, every experience becomes an opportunity for inner work, polishing up your stardust. Even in the most troubling situations, you can learn to choose peace of mind over fear and suffering. You can forgive and accept yourself and others if that is your intention.

While you can't change hurtful past experiences, you can change the relationship you have with those experiences and how you hold them in your heart and mind. I couldn't change the fact of my father's death, but I could change how I'd perceived myself as a victim for fifteen years, trapped in a prison of fear, anger, negativity, and self-pity. Psychedelic medicine helped me honor the constricted grief that needed to be expressed in order to deconstruct my "poor me" story. This freed me to create a new purpose. Now, my purpose is to do the best I can to live with an open heart and mind, attuned to the waves of guidance from Spirit, so I can align myself with Its will rather than the desires of my ego.

I don't always show up in this way, but I make an effort when I realize I am not being the person I want to be. I then rely on my standby mantra question: "How can I respond to the truth of what I am experiencing in a way that grows me in the directions I want to grow (toward the qualities of consciousness and being I want in my life)?"

Key 4: Recognize and give gratitude for the experiences and the support you're given.

Indigenous elders teach that humble, receptive, and grateful attunement with the powers of creation provides a foundation for creating a meaningful life, no matter what conditions are around you. Be grateful for everything and everyone who brings you challenges, for the mirror they hold up and for the opportunity they give to see your ego-bound ways. In this perspective, every situation is part of that which supports your growth.

Your loved ones, too, are sources of support. A thirteen-year-old boy who participated in one of my quest rites of passage reported this about his experience: "I realized I am strong enough to face the world, not only because I am capable as a person but because I have a community supporting me. I am strong enough to face the world because I am loved."

If you feel lost at any point or uncertain how to proceed, you can call on the ancestors for guidance.

In Indigenous societies, ancestral wisdom is passed down in rites of passage. Maintaining a good connection with ancestor spirits is considered essential in living a good life. For many of us, this idea is not something we consider important, and so the connection is lost. We suffer unknowingly for this loss, missing out on support that could be helpful to us in precarious times of crisis, where there is no guarantee of our survival.

There may be ancestral wounds that need healing. It is never too late to send healing love, both giving and seeking forgiveness down the ancestral line. In this way, you can heal wounds from the past that have been passed down through generations, letting the buck stop with you.

Opening the door to a conscious, respectful relationship with your ancestors allows you to access their support when facing challenges. You can thank them for their prayers, ceremonies, and initiatory rites of passage, without which you might not be here. Regular gratitude offerings keep the channels open to their support.

In my early sixties, I was moved by changes in my body to write a book about aging, but I did not know how I could find the time to write and keep up with my regular client load. I happened to mention this in casual conversation with a friend from the Center for Attitudinal Healing, where we worked with children facing life-threatening illness.* She suggested I write up a grant proposal and send it to her. I did, but I did not hear back. I continued my work, feeling disappointed and with dashed hopes of writing the book.

Years later, in a moment of fear and desperation over my financial situation, I stomped over to my ancestor altar and raised a pleading voice. "Ancestors, if you are really out there, if you are listening, thank you for my life, but right now I am feeling frantic. I don't have the money to pay our bills. I don't know what to do. Please help!"

On the verge of tears, I finished my plea, sprinkled a pinch of tobacco on the photos and objects of the altar, then walked downstairs to my home office, wondering if I was fooling myself and wasting my time. I looked at the pile of bills on my desk, shaking my head in despair. A few minutes later, I heard a thump outside my door.

"It's today's mail!" Andrea shouted.

Fearful to see even more bills, I anxiously picked up the letters lying at the bottom of the steps. Among the advertisements, requests for donations, and a few magazines, there was a letter from an old friend. Curiosity piqued, I opened the envelope, revealing a folded piece of stationary. As I unfolded it, a smaller piece of paper fell to the floor.

Intrigued, I picked up the paper and read its contents. To my astonishment, it was a check made out to me for twenty thousand dollars! I couldn't believe what I was seeing. Was this a mistake or some kind of joke? I hurried upstairs and showed it to Andrea, seeking her opinion. We both confirmed that it was indeed real, with my name clearly writ-

---

*See my book *Do They Celebrate Christmas in Heaven?* (published by Wakan Press in 1998) to learn more about this work.

ten on it. In that precise moment, I felt an overwhelming certainty that this was the work of my ancestors.

Moved by gratitude, I walked over to my ancestor altar and spoke softly, acknowledging their role in this unexpected blessing. "Wow, this is unbelievable. You work swiftly! Thank you, thank you so much!"

The unexpected gift allowed me to take time off from retreats, private practice, and consulting work to pursue this latest assignment in alignment with my purpose of bringing more love into the world. While skeptics may write off the timing of the surprise gift as mere coincidence, for me it was crystal clear. I had prayed to my ancestor spirits for assistance, and almost instantly the assistance arrived in the form of this remarkable and unexpected gift. When we open ourselves to the spirit world of our ancestors, miracles can unfold. It's important to trust the process. Sometimes, what may initially seem like a disastrous situation can unexpectedly pave the way for a miraculous outcome in the next moment.

The journey to purpose calls for acknowledging your needs and desires. What is calling you? If you deny or don't acknowledge what you want, the desire will only grow stronger. So instead, embrace it, own it as a genuine desire. Then, strategize on how you can skillfully, fruitfully, and successfully work toward achieving it. However, do so with humility, recognizing the presence of an invisible wisdom beyond your ego-based awareness, that knows what you truly need. Listen attentively for its guidance. Release attachment to your desired outcome, and remain open, flexible, and adaptable. Let go with faith and trust, opening yourself to yet unseen possibilities that may surpass your wildest dreams. There's a chance you could be wrong about what you think you need, and miss out on what is truly best.

Show up and do your part in pursuing what you feel called to do, but stay open to the mysteries of life. Surrender to an outcome that serves the highest good for all, releasing your personal will to the greater wisdom and cosmic flow that permeates the universe and resides within you.

Surrender is not about giving up in defeat, closing down, or retreating. It is about moving forward by consciously choosing to release yourself to something higher and greater than yourself. Here is a Sufi story that illustrates the transformative power of letting go:

> *Once, a stream flowed effortlessly through the country, navigating around rocks and through mountains. However, its journey came to a halt when it encountered a vast desert. Despite numerous attempts to cross it, the stream found that its waters quickly vanished into the sand. Overwhelmed by disappointment, it felt there was no way to continue its course.*
>
> *Then a voice came on the wind: "If you stay the way you are, you cannot cross the sands, you cannot become more than a quagmire. To go further you will have to lose yourself."*
>
> *"But if I lose myself," the stream cried, "I will never know what I'm supposed to be."*
>
> *"Oh, on the contrary," said the voice. "If you lose yourself, you will become more than you ever dreamed you could be."*
>
> *So the stream surrendered to the dying sun . . . and the clouds into which it formed were carried by the raging wind for many miles. Once it had crossed the desert, the stream poured down from the skies, fresh and clean and full of the energy that comes from storms.*

If you are older and haven't found your purpose at this late stage, I encourage you to read my book *Fruitful Aging*, where you'll discover stories of individuals who found their purpose in their golden years. For some of us, our purpose may not reveal itself until later in life. Regardless of your age, don't hesitate to continue searching. Here are some reflection questions to assist you in navigating toward your purpose. Take a moment to ponder them and see what insights arise:

- ♦ I came to Earth in this time and place so that I can _____.
- ♦ One problematic pattern I was born to understand that will keep recurring until I understand and master it is _____.
- ♦ What feels unfinished or incomplete about my life is _____. What I might be able to do about it now is _____.

♦ What my heart tells me is most important about how to live the remaining years of my life is _____.

You may also find it helpful in your quest for purpose to check in with your ancestor spirits, to see what they might suggest. One way to do this is to make an ancestor altar in your home, by doing the following:

Designate a special section on a shelf or table, and place pictures of family members who have died and other objects that remind you of your ancestors.

Each morning upon awakening, go to the altar and give thanks to your ancestors, known and unknown.

Offer a prayer, a song, words, a chant, some incense, fresh flowers, anything that expresses gratitude.

Tell them you seek their guidance about your life's purpose. (Watch your dreams, an answer may come through your dreaming.)

As you begin to discover and live your purpose, you will thrive from the inside out. You will make a positive difference in this chaotic world. Whenever I paddle or kayak out into the ocean and witness another boat passing by, I notice how they all leave a wake, creating ripples that travel across the water until they merge with the vast sea. What kind of wake will you leave behind?

CHAPTER 11

YOU MATTER

When a new world is born, the old turns itself inside out,
to cleanse and prepare for a new beginning.

PETER BLUE, NATIVE POET

In the fall of 2018, California's most devastating and lethal fire thus far burned down an entire town in rural Northern California, ironically named Paradise. For ten days, smoke from the Paradise fire was carried by winds hundreds of miles south to the San Francisco Bay Area, where I live, concealing the sun behind a veil of smoke so thick the sky during the day and stars at night became invisible. People stayed in their homes, yearning for relief. If one ventured outside, they had to wear a mask to avoid choking. Burning eyes and lungs, nausea, and headaches became common plights. Many elderly and health-compromised individuals ended up hospitalized.

One day, during the peak of the dark, choking, smoke-filled air, a pressing need to replenish dwindling food and supplies propelled me out of my house. With my mask on, I opened the door and was stunned to find the sun invisible in broad daylight. Instead, an eerie, orange sky hung overhead, the air filled with the stench of burning chemicals. *This is like Armageddon, the end of the world,* I found myself thinking.

I am not an alarmist or pessimist, but this thought on that dismal day aligns with the words of the late futurist Barbara Marx Hubbard.

An outspoken wisdom elder of the conscious evolution movement, she poignantly wrote, "The eleventh hour is upon us. We're either on board or we'll be left behind. We are at the tip of the tipping point, humanity is about to evolve . . . or collapse."

In December 2020, the United Nations Secretary-General António Guterres spoke pointedly. "Dear friends," he began, "let's be clear: human activities are at the root of our descent toward chaos. We are waging war on nature. This is suicidal." He continued, "Nature always strikes back—and it is already doing so with growing force and fury. Making peace with nature is the defining task of the twenty-first century. It must be the top priority for everyone, everywhere."

Futurist Peter Russell, known for his groundbreaking thoughts on consciousness and the future of humanity, explains, "Breakthrough and breakdown are now two sides of the same coin. They are ramping up and coming to a head together. We have technology beyond our dreams in a world that's falling apart at the seams. In a hundred years we may be extinct—or well on our way to extinction." He laments the tragedy of humanity, a species with such unprecedented capacities, potentially nearing self-destruction.

Many Indigenous cultures have ancient prophecies that foretell these troubling times. In the mid-1960s I was fortunate to spend time with Hindu swamis including Satchitanada, Yogi Bajan, Muktananda, Bhaktivedanta, and numerous others, taking part in ceremony and ritual practices. Hindu metaphysics views time within a circle of ages, known as the yugas. Each yuga presents distinct themes and spiritual lessons for humanity. Thousands of years ago, Hindu cosmologists predicted our current time, calling it the "Age of the Kali Yuga." This cosmic cycle is marked by quarrel and strife, and spiritual degeneration due to human distance from God. In this age, virtue holds little value, passions run rampant, and society is rife with manipulation. Important knowledge is lost, leading to human migration in search of stable food sources. Animosity and violence escalate, and the feminine influence in civilization gradually disappears from history.

The Hopi Indians of Arizona also believe we are living in a time of crisis, known as the Fourth World. This time is characterized by purification manifesting as an increasingly erratic climate. Their ancient prophecies anticipated drastic earthquakes, tsunamis, hurricanes, tornadoes, record breaking flooding, wildfires, drought, and famine. Along with these natural catastrophes, a number of technological changes were foreseen to signal the end of the Fourth World.

These prophecies, made long before the first Europeans landed on American shores, predicted a time when a "gourd of ashes" would fall on the Earth. Today, we understand the catastrophic consequences of nuclear explosions: the destructive fallout of ashes and the

Guadalupe de la Cruz

lingering radioactive poison that persists for tens of thousands of years. Interestingly, Hopi prophecies alluded to "horseless wagons" traversing "black ribbons" (akin to modern day traffic on freeways), aerial vehicles navigating "roads in the heavens," and humans "living in the sky," which one could interpret as astronauts dwelling in space stations.

Decades later, those prophetic Hopi messages reverberated on a remote Huichol ranch in Mexico, recounted by Guadalupe de la Cruz. An esteemed elder, Guadalupe was a shamanic healer, singer, artist, and ceremonial leader, dedicating her life to preserving and transmitting the spiritual teachings of her forebears. Throughout our shared moments on her ranch, as well as during eleven strenuous three-hundred-mile pilgrimages to Wiricuta (a crucial part of my shamanic initiation), Guadalupe became a spiritual grandmother to me.

Incapable of having children, Guadalupe gave her nurturing energy to the many children of the rancho, and to others who came her way with respect, humility, and sincerity. Throughout the decades I knew her, up till her death in 1999, she always endeavored to honor and pass on the sacred medicine ways that had been passed on to her.

Upon returning from a pilgrimage, she gathered the children and teenagers of the rancho around the ceremonial fire and gently fed pieces of peyote to each one. "Eat this," she'd say warmly. "It will help you know your heart." Such a contrast with the Just Say No admonition in the United States at the time.

One warm afternoon, I sat with Grandmother in the shade of her *tuki*, a unique structure holding her ceremonial items. She told me that *Taupa*, Father Sun, was drawing nearer to Mother Earth to rouse "los gringos en el Norte" because we had lost touch with the fact that the Earth is alive. We had forgotten that the elements—fire, sky, rain, wind—are all living beings. We had lost the way to coexist respectfully with the Gods and Goddesses, thus creating problems for all. This wisdom was bestowed upon me long before the term "global warming" entered common parlance.

What Guadalupe said about Father Sun heating up the Earth, just as the Hopi and Hindu prophecies predicted, seems to be unfolding.

We find ourselves in an era of drastic systemic collapse, a purification of sorts. I grapple with despair when I consider the future. I am now an elderly man who has led a fulfilling life, but what about the hopes and dreams I harbor for my grandchildren? What about yours? What future awaits them? Is it too late for us to act? Are we destined to be consumed by fear, depression, sadness, anger, bitterness, grief, and despair? What responses might serve us best in the face of these daunting challenges? What qualities of consciousness and action give us the best shot at navigating this precarious time and fostering a quality of life that makes it worth living?

> *Psychedelic Shamanic Wisdom Warrior consciousness lives in the awareness that you are more than just your ego identity, your stories, or your physical body with its wounds and trauma.*

Let's start with respect, needed now more than ever—the kind of respect called for by fifteenth-century Chinese poet Teo Lei: "Respect for the kind of intelligence that enables a grass seed to grow grass, a cherry stone to make cherries."

Psychedelic shamanism offers practices, such as vision quests and carefully planned journeys with sacred power plants, that cultivate this kind of respect. The following prayer by Oglala holy man Black Elk encapsulates this respect.

"Oh Wakan Tanka, Sacred Mystery, Great Spirit, teach me to walk upon the soft Earth as a relative to all that live. Sweeten my heart and fill me with light. Grant me the strength to comprehend and eyes to perceive."

In order to have eyes that truly see, there must be a shift from the perceptual and cognitive lens that views and interprets the world through a materialist paradigm, which falsely assumes separation, to a psychedelic perspective that embraces and connects with the creative wisdom and power of the universe. This shift brings about a clearer understanding of how reality actually operates, recognizing that all of creation is interwoven in a sacred web of oneness. Survival is dependent on cooperative rather than competitive interactions among people, and with the generative forces of nature that sustain our lives.

Psychedelic Shamanic Wisdom Warrior consciousness lives in the awareness that you are more than just your ego identity, your stories, or your physical body with its wounds and trauma. Psychedelic Shamanic Wisdom Warrior consciousness acknowledges and embraces the essence of your deeper being as luminosity, for you are a divine spark, an integral part of the infinite, unconditional light and love of the universe. This realization became evident to me during my first psychedelic vision, in 1966, when my perception expanded to a wider bandwidth, allowing me to experience divinity for the first time. This was a transformative moment in my life, as biologist Rupert Sheldrake eloquently expresses, "To fully realize our humanity, it is necessary to recognize our divinity."

Some years ago, as described at the beginning of this book, I was driving and listening to a podcast by astrophysicist Neil deGrasse Tyson, when he stated that "We are stardust brought to life."

At that precise moment, a beam of sunlight burst through the windshield, illuminating my car with its brilliance despite the otherwise cloudy sky. *It's true, I understand it now. We are stardust brought to life.*

Today, science has revealed that the trillions of atoms in our bodies were forged through nuclear reactions in supernova explosions of ancient stars. These atoms were recycled through the births and deaths of more stars until they eventually formed our solar system and everything within it. Tyson's statement is accurate: we are all stardust that came to Earth and, over billions of years, evolved to human primates with a prefrontal cortex capable of contemplating ideas like the ones you are reading about right here and now.

In contemplating the notion of stardust brought to life, I recalled the Hawaiian word "ohana," which means extended family, and it suddenly occurred to me that all human beings are members of a Starlight Ohana simply by virtue of our birth. The very building blocks of our physical bodies are composed of stardust energy from the sun, and we are all fueled by the life-force stardust energy it provides.

The starlight that poured through my windshield that day reaffirmed what I'd learned on my LSD journey decades ago: that our deepest essence is as one with the infinite, unconditional love I felt emanating from Christ's heart when he prayed for forgiveness for the soldiers who were impaling him on the cross, recognizing that they were asleep in the illusion of separation. In the deepest level of our being, we are one with the cosmic consciousness of stardust, with the activating, creating, wisdom power of the universe—with God. If the word "God" is triggering for you, feel free to replace it with a term that resonates with your understanding.

If we trace our roots back far enough, we find our ancestors living within a covenant of understanding of interconnectedness. They knew that everything was alive with Spirit at its core. Consequently, they treated all aspects of creation with respect. They also recognized the necessity of taking other lives, be it animal or plant, in order to sustain their own. However, they grasped something that modern society seems to have forgotten: the sacredness of reciprocity. They understood that to maintain balance in an ecosystem, one cannot simply take without giving back in some measure. Rituals and ceremonies emerged as ways to express gratitude and restore this balance, both individually and communally.

In the civilizations of modernity, driven by an out of control consumer capitalist economic system that prioritizes material wealth, acquisition, and profits over people, this ancient understanding of right-relationship within the covenant of life has been lost. Mainstream consciousness today emphasizes the pursuit of personal gain and the accumulation of possessions, often at the expense of others. There is little awareness of the importance of reciprocity and giving back, aside from the occasional observance of thanks-giving.

The intertwined crises of today call for a reweaving of the sacred covenant. We are called upon to discern what needs to be discarded and what needs to be replaced in order for humanity to meet its collective needs in a harmonious and balanced manner within the interlocking systems of nature. We are summoned to embody and live as Psychedelic Shamanic Wisdom Warriors who recognize the sanctity of creation, the inherent holiness within ourselves, and the profound sacredness of life itself. We must relearn how to live in a holy manner, integrating the insights and benefits of science and technology with the wisdom of Indigenous spirituality that remains alive to this day. It is imperative that we establish an economic system that serves life, rather than one that enriches a select few at the expense of others and the well-being of our planet, Mother Earth. We must awaken to our true nature, our shared luminosity as stardust, and live wisely from that understanding.

The Japanese word *kensho* refers to a glimpse of our true nature. Today we need not just a glimpse, a peak experience, or momentary opening—we need sustained attunement to the high intelligence of psychedelic shamanic cosmic consciousness with which to transform a fear-based world to a love-based one. This is the work of Wisdom Warriors.

Spiritual teachers, mystics, and Indigenous belief systems around the world have been telling us for eons that the illusionary perception of separation is not true; underlying the appearance of separation, we are all one. In cultures that place primary value on material acquisition and surface appearances, these voices usually go unheeded and are largely ignored.

Today, quantum physics, the study of the smallest aspects of reality we can measure, is fortunately presenting evidence that supports what these ancient voices have been trying to bring to our attention for so long.

It will take a critical mass of Wisdom Warriors who understand the tricky illusionary aspect of the universe to shift our current toxic way of living on Mother Earth to a healthy, stable rejuvenating one. The good news is, there are growing numbers of people, young and old, who see through the illusion of separation. Hopefully you are one of those people, or will be soon.

Evolutionary pressure is pushing us to forge a new vision, a new way of living based on love. Each of us has the power to forge such a vision. What you think, what you feel, what you say, and what you do has an impact that not only affects you—its energy creates an impact in the larger field because everything is connected. You make a difference. What kind of difference? That is up to you.

Through psychedelic shamanic attunement with the creative cosmic-intelligence powers that give and sustain life, you can show up in the world as a conscious change agent, a spiritual activist, a Wisdom Warrior shapeshifting fear to love, injustice to justice, racist beliefs, actions, and institutional policies toward fairness and equal opportunity for all.

When there is oppression or injustice done to any of the human family, hurtful behavior toward whales, elephants, butterflies, bees, monkeys, cows, sheep, pigs, octopuses, horses, or dolphins, or hurtful behavior to the oceans, jungles, forests, rivers, and soil of the land—our souls know it and cry out in pain.

Soul pain comes out as suffering through frustration, fear, anxiety, disgust, anger, despair, depression, and feelings of hopelessness and powerlessness in response to the chaos and uncertainty of our times. All aspects of suffering need to be faced and worked with using compassion and empathy, but awareness of suffering needs to also be a springboard to action.

Indigenous activist and author Leanne Simpson, in her book, *Dancing on Our Turtle's Back: Stories of Nishnaabeg Re-Creation, Resurgence and a New Emergence*, points us in the right direction:

> Figure out how to live responsibly and be accountable to the next seven generations of people, relearning how to derive happiness and satisfaction from sources other than shopping. Our ancestors didn't prioritize accumulating wealth or material possessions. Instead, they invested their energy in meaningful and authentic relationships. It was the quality of those relationships—not their quantity or material possessions—that formed the foundation of their happiness.

Regardless of the challenges or circumstances we face today, we possess the ability to heal the human-caused disasters occurring worldwide. Together, as an extended Starlight Ohana family, we have the capacity to work cooperatively to create a healthy, just, peaceful, beautiful, equitable, rejuvenating, Win-Win World of harmony and balance for All. This can be achieved if enough of us are willing to do the necessary work and embrace our roles as Wisdom Warriors.

While ancient prophecies and modern climate warnings paint a bleak future, it is the responsibility of the Wisdom Warriors who understand the potential accomplishments of cooperative groups with shared goals to step forward and keep the flame of hope burning in dark times.

When hearts and minds unite with a shared intention, their power surpasses that of individuals acting alone. Consider the laws of wave mechanics: when two waves converge, their combined strength is four times greater than that of a single wave; ten waves are a hundred times as powerful. Since thoughts are waves of energy, when a sufficient number of people focus positive energy on the same thoughts, they can eventually reach a critical mass that induces morphic shifts, allowing significant changes to occur rapidly. If your doubting mind believes that getting people with differing beliefs to cooperate on a mass scale is an impossible task, consider this:

Every time you embark on a journey, notice that each individual on the road is operating a steel container weighing thousands of pounds, is moving at high speeds, and is constantly making split-second decisions. Remarkably, these actions are coordinated with countless other drivers who, through unspoken agreement, cooperate with one another. This system functions because all drivers adhere to specific rules of the road, regardless of their differences in nationality, religion, ethnicity, color, size, shape, sexual identity, or political beliefs. This illustrates what can be achieved when there is a collective commitment to a common goal: arriving safely at the desired destination—a goal no one can accomplish solely on their own.

Another inspiring example of what can happen when a critical mass of people consciously agrees on what is of utmost importance is the story of the Berlin Wall. Erected by Russia during the Cold War to prevent residents of Soviet-occupied East Berlin from seeking freedom in West Berlin, the wall was heavily fortified with barbed wire fences and guarded by soldiers. Those attempting to overcome it were met with deadly force. Then, one peaceful day, without any violence, the seemingly impenetrable wall crumbled. Why? A shift in consciousness reached a tipping point where the collective agreement emerged: it was time for the wall to be dismantled.

STEP FOUR

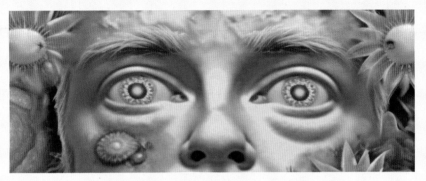

The Wisdom
Warrior Path

TOOLS AND TECHNIQUES FOR PSYCHEDELIC
SHAMANIC WISDOM WARRIORS

Huichol yarn painting depicting spiritual wisdom

CHAPTER 12

TRAITS OF WISDOM WARRIORS

Wisdom is not something to acquire, but a way of being.
ALAN WATTS

E volutionary pressure urges humanity to develop a planetary consciousness in harmony with the natural cycles of life. This consciousness entails a new way of perceiving, existing, and living, which is
beautifully exemplified in models provided by Indigenous spirituality.
Indeed, such a shift in worldview may be the only feasible solution to
the daunting challenges of climate change and the pervasive pandemics
of disease, injustice, depression, suicide, and racism. If we fail to con-
ceptualize and embody a new vision for our collective future, we risk
rendering that future unviable.

Each of us holds the power to contribute to this vision and to
become a Wisdom Warrior. Your thoughts, your emotions, your words,
and your actions have a ripple effect; they don't merely influence you
but extend to impact the larger field. You have the capacity to effect
change. The nature of the difference you make, however, remains your
choice.

To instigate change on a planetary scale, we need a critical mass of
Wisdom Warriors committed to transitioning our current detrimental
way of life to a more sustainable and regenerative one. While the term

"warrior" may have negative connotations for many, particularly due to its association with male-dominated violence, it also embodies positive attributes such as discernment, courage, commitment, and discipline. As Wisdom Warriors, we stand up for justice and protect the most vulnerable among us.

Wisdom differs from knowledge. Knowledge encompasses facts and ideas, whereas wisdom is the capacity to discern which aspects of knowledge can pragmatically apply to your life and, more importantly, how to live out those truths, particularly under pressure. While knowledge is intellectually attained, wisdom must be lived—otherwise, it remains abstract and powerless.

Wisdom involves learning the lessons of the revelatory universe that we live in and that lives in us. It helps us to transition, as psychologist and author Bill Plotkin suggests, from "our first adulthood," rooted in ego, to "our second adulthood," which is soul based. Wisdom encompasses understanding the teachings of impermanence and recognizing that the soul's nourishment can't be found in material possessions.

Innovative research conducted at prestigious institutions such as Princeton, MIT, and Stanford, among others, echoes what Indigenous people have known for millennia: the universe is connected by a vast quantum energy field. Thoughts and consciousness generate an energy force that, when combined with the focus of others on the same intention, can engender significant change in the world.

The Global Consciousness Project, based at Princeton University, is an international, multidisciplinary collaboration of scientists and engineers. This initiative, which collects data continuously from across the globe, posits that "[. . .] when a great event synchronizes the feelings of millions of people, our network of Random Number Generators becomes subtly structured. We calculate one in a trillion odds that the effect is due to chance. The evidence suggests an emerging noosphere or the unifying field of consciousness described by sages across cultures."

These times call for Psychedelic Shamanic Wisdom Warriors who strive to live as if each day is a "great event"—serving Spirit with joy, grace, and gratitude.

Quantum theoretician Henry Stapp elucidates the influence of thought on the field of consciousness: "[. . .] the new physics presents prima facie evidence that our human thoughts are linked to nature by nonlocal connections: what a person chooses to do in one region seems immediately to effect what is true elsewhere in the universe" (from "Future Visions" by Henry Stapp, August 21, 2000).

Our thoughts . . . are effective.

QUALITIES OF WISDOM WARRIORS

Wisdom Warriors skillfully use the power of focused mind for healing, transformation, and working to create a healthy, peaceful, and just world for everyone. Psychedelic shamanic practices grow Wisdom Warriors. The Dalai Lama serves as an exemplary Wisdom Warrior with a psychedelic consciousness—without the use of psychoactive substances; his tradition and training guided him.

He advocates for a spiritual revolution, a "radical shift from our habitual self-centered preoccupation toward a consideration for the wider community of beings to which we are connected, and for actions that recognize the interests of others along with our own." He emphasizes the need for "wisdom shifts in motivation from serving personal desires to serving purposes higher than ego gratification. Not my will, but Thy will. Not I, but we."

Wisdom Warriors adeptly navigate through challenging and complex times with an open heart. Cultivate resilience and endurance to persevere, keeping the flame of love, kindness, generosity, and hope alive even when faced with great adversities threatening to extinguish it.

Wisdom Warriors understand that the most profound battle is the spiritual struggle within the human heart. Being a Wisdom Warrior isn't about aggression or violence, but rather a confrontation with internal adversaries whose energies seek to close the heart.

Wisdom Warriors undertake a disciplined practice that enhances mindfulness. This allows you to move beyond ego to access a larger bandwidth of consciousness and power and grow the qualities of being you want to show up more consistently in your life. Without a practice that applies a clear, disciplined focus of intention, the energy of intension becomes weak, easily dispersed, and entirely susceptible to competing distractions, akin to a rudderless boat aimlessly tossed about by superior forces.

Wisdom Warriors treat challenges as opportunities for growth. Reframe challenges as vehicles of opportunity to go deeper, in order to find the medicine teaching/healing trying to come through the situation. Just as coal doesn't become a diamond without pressure, and iron doesn't turn to fine steel without enduring heat, humans cannot grow without facing trials.

Wisdom Warriors understand the balance of gratitude. For all that is given and all that is taken, there must be genuine expression of gratitude and reciprocation of appreciation, or else disharmony breeds, asking for trouble.

Wisdom Warriors strive to understand the root of their reactivity and suffering. Stories born from an ego identity characterized by self-importance, entitlement, attachment, aversion, ignorance, arrogance, absence of presence, unnecessary time pressures, and taking matters personally will cause suffering. The mission is to extinguish these energy patterns, replacing them with those that nurture the soul, not the ego.

Wisdom Warriors befriend mortality as an ally, using its inevitability to perform each action as though it might be their last—for one day, it will be. The concept of dying is alarming when one is excessively attached to a fearful ego and physical body, unfortified by the practice of letting go. The shift from identifying with the body and ego to recognizing one's spirit, the true essence, requires relinquishing control.

Wisdom Warriors are ambassadors of love. Channel unconditional love to all interactions by showing kindness, care, and generosity, thus raising the vibrational level of your surroundings. Don't seek love from others; instead, radiate love to others, serving as conduits for the universe's love that flows with every breath.

Wisdom Warriors bring beauty to the world through creative expression. Listen to the soft urges of creativity that come through your body, your intuition, your feelings, and your dreams. Listen to how those creative energies want to be expressed—drawing or painting, movement or sound, song, dance, or playing an instrument, sculpting, creating something, or scribbling on a large pad of paper with crayons or felt-tipped pens, doodling or writing stream-of-consciousness poetry—letting the energy out however it wants.

It can be a fun adventure to not know what will come forth. Open to the mystery of creation. Step out of ego's comfort zone. Honor what your creative flow is asking from you. Don't shut down in fear, judgment, or negative thoughts: "I can't sing. I can't draw. I can't play the piano. I'm not a writer. I'm not a poet. I'm not a dancer. I'm not creative."

This kind of thinking clogs your pipes, and nothing good comes from that. Jump in. Heed the call for expression from your deeper self, and it will reward you. You are a writer, dancer, singer, and poet—in your own unique way. Release comparisons and evaluations. Just let creativity flow. More creativity will come, and your life will be enriched.

Wisdom Warriors strengthen their body/mind container. Cultivate physical, mental, emotional, and spiritual well-being through harmonious alignment with nature both within and without. Just as the mind needs training and maintenance, so too does the soul need regular nourishment, the heart tender loving care, and the body right nutrition, right exercise, and right rest and relaxation.

Meditation, breathwork, prayer, ritual, spending time in silence listening, centering, grounding, and engaging in present relaxation are integral aspects of Wisdom Warrior practice. Activities such as yoga, aikido, T'ai Chi, and Qigong, along with psychotherapy and mindfully engaged pursuits such as dancing, running, hiking, walking, biking, mountain climbing, rock climbing, swimming, paddle boarding, kayaking, cross-country skiing, and weight training are all practices that can strengthen the container of Self. Push beyond your comfort zones, working holistically on your body, mind, and spirit.

It's essential to maintain a good stretching routine, especially as we age. This practice complements strengthening routines by promoting flexibility, fluidity, and adaptability, attributes critical for aging bodies.

Wisdom Warriors befriend their shadow. Like a hunter, stalk the contents of your unconscious—dreams, body symptoms such as aches, pains, and wounds, and reactive trigger points—to gain awareness of your shadow self. Watch for leaks in your energy field where you lose power, weaken, or constrict the flow of creative energy. This could manifest in complaining, self-pity, craving recognition and acclaim, worrying, and harshly judging yourself or others. Venture to the introspective depths and seek out the roots of what triggers you. These challenging incidents are not accidental—they are tests in your spiritual journey, prompting the deep work you are avoiding.

Challenges can seem overwhelming, but the goal is not to strive for perfection, as this only sets the stage for frustration and failure. Instead, the aim is harmony and balance within the entirety of your being, and with "all your relations."

Wisdom Warriors hunt, gather, and store power. Power is associated with the capacity to manifest change or make things happen. The greatest power is obtained through a relationship with forces greater than ourselves—nature's powers such as wind, ocean tides and waves, and the life giving force that emerges from Mother Earth each spring. Ultimately, this power is the Source power of all creation, whatever name you identify with it—God, Goddess, Holy Mother, Holy Spirit, Tao, Great Spirit, Sacred Mystery, Creator, etcetera.

But how can this power be harnessed?

Hunt for this power by opening yourself to its presence, cultivating relationship by dedicating quality time to expressing gratitude for the bountiful gifts it provides. Grace grows where gratitude flows. To gain more grace, express more gratitude.

Power can be stored in your solar plexus, place of light—what the Japanese refer to as *hara*, and the Chinese *dan t'ien*. Think of this accumulation of power as making regular deposits to your bank account, ensuring you have the resources to cover expenses when needed.

Wisdom Warriors establish shamanic connection with their power animals—totem or spirit animals that serve as lifelong partners, provided the relationship is respected and nurtured. Traditionally, individuals become aware of their totem spirit through a dream, vision quest, pilgrimage to a sacred place, or an encounter in the physical world where the animal communicates its presence and willingness for partnership.

A power animal bestows its wisdom, strength, and medicine to assist you in your life. This spirit animal acts as an intermediary between the spirit and physical worlds, helping you recognize and realize the full spectrum of your multidimensional being. Like any relationship, the bond with your power animal can flourish or wither depending on the attention and energy it's given. To welcome the animal spirit and make full use of its gifts, acknowledge its presence and create a welcoming space for it in your consciousness and life. Invite the totem spirit into your body, mind, and spirit so it can impart its wisdom. Perhaps it might reveal a power song or a power dance, enabling you to understand better its unique abilities to assist in your life.

It's important to regularly honor your power animal spirit by expressing gratitude, singing songs, offering tobacco or cornmeal, playing music, or through other means that genuinely acknowledge its existence.

I begin each day by expressing thanks to the power animal allies who have come into my life during periods of fasting in the mountains, in dreams, and through visions. I pray for their lives and their families, and offer gifts to nourish their spirits. Often, I sing and drum the songs they've taught me. When faced with challenges during a psychedelic journey, vision quest, or in everyday life, I'm confident that calling upon them will yield positive responses, granting me access to the wisdom, guidance, and power best suited for the situation.

My initial vision quest in the Sierra introduced me to my first power animal, the deer. Subsequent quests welcomed other power animals—the bear, the eagle, the coyote, the frog, the black panther, the butterfly, and the rattlesnake. Some arrived through dreams, others during psychedelic medicine journeys, and some through physical encounters.

Without the help of my totem allies, I'm not sure I would still be alive to write this book. The same kind of help is available to you if you seek out and create good working relationships with your totem helpers.

Wisdom Warriors, when called to do so, respect psychedelic substances and honor all involved spirits with gratitude, humility and joy.

Wisdom Warriors comprehend their obligation to serve as spiritual activists. Strive to cultivate a healthy, peaceful, fair, caring, and mutually beneficial world for all—the only type of world that truly works. Connect with the wisdom power of the universe, staying vigilant to bust limiting thoughts about what is possible. Remain aware of limiting thoughts, letting them pass without empowering them.

Wisdom Warriors take action. It's impossible to grasp what's possible until you show up and follow your soul's calling. Consider Gandhi: a simple Hindu man dressed in a loincloth who showed up for India, initiating a nonviolent movement that ultimately overthrew British rule and altered history's course.

Wisdom Warriors cultivate constructive relationships with their emotions, using them as allies on their journey of enlightenment and growth. Befriend anxiety, fear, anger, shame, envy, guilt, remorse, and judgments by bringing awareness to the underlying thought patterns and stories that create suffering, and releasing them with conscious out breaths. Face these emotions bravely, using them to identify inhibitions, narratives you tell yourself, and detrimental patterns causing distress. Once you gain insight, exhale these feelings, releasing what no longer benefits you.

Wisdom Warriors elevate their divine sparks through a clear channel to their higher selves, polishing their path with sunlight's stardust and serving as vessels for this refined light to radiate to all they encounter. Seize each moment, using it to embrace the gift of presence—and the presence of gifts—that emerge from an open heart and recognition of the love you embody.

Wisdom Warriors listen for the gentle voice of Spirit's guidance. Communicate with Spirit by listening through your body, emotions, intuition, dreams, and imagination, as well as through unsolicited coyote trickster schemes aiming to expand awareness beyond ego drives and rational mind constraints.

Wisdom Warriors strive to remain open, humble, receptive, and attentive to everyone and everything. Remain aware that the sacred mystery is always present and always seeking to bring through the fullest blossoming for greatest good. But it takes work to bring this blossoming through—and that is why you are in whatever situation you are in, to show up and do your part to make the greatest benefit for the greatest good happen.

Wisdom Warriors stand against wrongdoings in the sacred web of life. Stand against injustice, prejudice, racism, discrimination, violence, and harmful institutional policies. Advocate for equality, justice, peace, beauty, kindness, caring, and generosity. Inaction only reinforces the continuation of destructive systems, beliefs, values, and behaviors that cause and perpetuate today's social and environmental issues.

Wisdom Warriors heed the wisdom of the heart to *hana pono*, a Hawaiian phrase meaning, "do the right thing." Let your heart guide you, not your ego. Live your integrity serving higher will and greatest good for all.

Wisdom Warriors practice the art of releasing critical judgments that close the heart and obstruct the flow of love. As singer Bob Seger says in one of his songs, "Keep your heart as open as a shrine. You'll sail the perfect line!"

Extend unconditional love to others rather than conditional love, given with strings attached, such as wanting a person to change in some way in order to receive your love.

Wisdom Warriors identify with the divinity they embody. You are divine sparks of stardust brought to Earth to spread love.

Wisdom Warriors know that love is for giving, and so are forgiving to themselves and others, holding their hearts open, free from judgment. They refrain from attempting to control others, opting instead to accept them as they are. If others engage in harmful, destructive behavior fueled by prejudice, racist, or white supremacist ideology or ignorance, it indicates they are lost in the illusion of separation. This does not mean that hurtful acts are OK, so yes, judge the actions for what they are, but do not judge the being of another, for then you judge yourself as well, and fuel the false identity of self as separate from others. While harmful actions must be halted, judging the being of a person for their ignorance or pain can close your heart and harm you. In the game of life, the one who loves most wins.

Wisdom Warriors utilize shamanic practices for accessing psychedelic consciousness to *tikkun olam*, a Hebrew phrase meaning to "heal the wounds of the world." By working on consciousness and advocating for systemic change in policies and actions that harm individuals and the planet, we can heal planetary "wounds."

Wisdom Warriors collaborate to devise new structural systems that address shared human needs independent of consumer growth and expansion. Contribute to the construction of cooperative, symbiotic systems that harmoniously promote the flourishing of all in a healthy way. In the shared lifeboat of existence, exclusion of any group from fair resource allocation risks sinking us all.

Wisdom Warriors work diligently to cultivate resilience across all aspects of their existence—mental, emotional, cognitive, physical,

and spiritual. Adopt a mindset rooted in the Three Cs: Commitment, Challenge, and Control.

Commitment: An ever-growing body of scientific research implies that possessing a purpose in life is not just fulfilling, but life sustaining. To what purpose can you commit that transcends merely serving your ego?

Challenge: Psychedelic Shamanic Wisdom Warriors use triggering situations as challenges for finding and bringing through good medicine, shifting the state of victimhood to empowering efficacy, using the trigger to foster healthy growth.

Control: Differentiate what you have control over (your responses to situations, your intentions, and your focus of attention) from what you do not have control over (how people respond to or think of you, or the outcome of situations). Be a love giver instead of a love seeker. Control your energy state and strengthen your emotional immune system, moving toward high-level wellness.

Practice the Three Cs and other qualities of the Wisdom Warrior to polish up your stardust and actualize your highest potential. Become a clean, clear, open channel for Spirit's light and love to flow through you to the world, working toward fullest blossoming and greatest good for all.

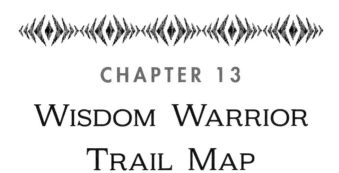

CHAPTER 13

WISDOM WARRIOR
TRAIL MAP

Here are some of the exercises, tools, and techniques that helped me on my journey to becoming a Psychedelic Shamanic Wisdom Warrior:

CONNECTING WITH NATURE

Go outside. Find a serene outdoor spot where you can connect with the Earth. Be still and allow your mind to quiet down while relaxing your body. Open your awareness to your senses, tuning in to the sensations, feelings, sounds, sights, and observations around you. Pay close attention to everything that comes your way. Take off your shoes and stand barefoot on the ground. Grounding. Earthing. Direct your focus to the soles of your feet and feel the sensations they pick up. Allow yourself to simply be present on the Earth, taking in the breath of life. Observe without any need for action. Be fully aware of your direct experience. Engage your senses. Feel. Listen. Observe.

Express gratitude to each of the seven directions, following the Native American medicine wheel tradition: to the East, South, West, North, and the powers above, below, and within. From the depths of your heart, send out gratitude and maintain a patient presence to see what insights you can glean about the wisdom of your surroundings. Offer thanks to the ancestral spirits of the land beneath your feet.

Pray for humanity to awaken from the nightmare of separation and to embrace the interconnectedness of all life.

Directing gratitude energy to the Earth beneath your feet, feel energy rising from the Earth into your body. If you remain still enough, you may even sense the Earth's rhythmic breath. Ask yourself, "Is this ground I'm standing on merely an inanimate object, devoid of life force?"

Hold a rock, feel its composition with your fingers. Pay attention to what you become aware of as you hold it. Rocks are composed of atoms and molecules. These molecules and atoms vibrate, representing energy in motion. See if you can slow down enough to sense the vibrating energy of the rock.

The vibration you feel is a form of communication, even though the rock is not alive in the biological sense. Indigenous people believe that the "rock people" are the oldest beings, and that they hold the history of the planet. Can you lower your vibrational rate enough to sense what the rock you are holding is communicating? Try asking the rock, the Earth beneath your feet, and the expressions of nature around you for guidance on how you can contribute your gifts to the awakening of human consciousness. Listen with your heart, body, and feelings. Take note of what comes back to you through this type of listening. Perhaps mainstream culture would benefit from broadening its notions of communication beyond what it considers "alive."

If more people came to see the "inanimate" Earth as alive, recognizing that her gifts enable us to live, then more of us might cooperatively develop ways of meeting our collective needs that are not harmful to life, but instead are in respectful, harmonious relationship with it. This alone would begin to heal the soul wound of alienation many of us suffer from—a wound that leads to the pervasive violence in modern society.

EXERCISE

◆ Polish Up Your Stardust

+ Every morning, take a few minutes to connect with the light of the sun, or the light of a candle if you are inside.

- As you look toward the light, let your eyes go soft.
- Notice how you can actually see beams of light flowing to you. Take it in.
- Breathing in, fill up your tank with this life force fuel.
- Feel what you are thankful for in that precise moment.
- Breathe out, extending gratitude from your heart in whatever way feels right for you, be it through words, song, movement, or perhaps with music.
- Repeat: "I am a Sacred, Worthy, Luminous Being. I am loved. I am love. And my love is for giving and receiving. I Live Love Now."
- Use the light flowing into you as fuel to energize your ability to shine your love ever brighter and stronger to the world and to all your interactions of daily living. Do it now.

CREATING THE FUTURE

Take responsibility for the vision of the future you would like to see. This future starts in your mind as an act of imagination, a seed/kernel of an idea. Imagine what you want the world to look like, to be like. Take your time with this. See it in detail. Get into it.

When you have a clear image in mind, energize that picture by imagining that it already exists in physical reality, that it has already been achieved and is working as you see it in your mind's eye. Feel the gratitude, the joy, the happiness you would experience if the world were actually functioning as the manifestation of your vision. Give thanks for it being so. When you feed your vision with this kind of positive energy on a regular basis, its vibratory power strengthens. It may be "all in your mind," but if you keep it up, you will be guided to actionable steps toward making it come true on the material plane.

EXERCISE

❮❯ *Reflection Questions*

- How can I create a response to the challenges in my life and the challenges of the times, that grows me in the direction I want to grow?

- How can I show up to support a new vision of living based on love working for social, environmental, and economic justice for all?
- How can I play my part in helping to deconstruct societal ills that are harmful to the Earth, to animals, and to people—especially white supremacy racism woven into the institutions that privilege Caucasians while discriminating against Indigenous people and other People of Color? How might the work be done from an open, kind heart, instead of from bitterness, anger, and blame?

POWER OF PRAYER

One of the most effective ways to raise your vibrational energy and reach higher realms is through prayer. However, it's important to note that the term "prayer" can have different meanings for different people. Allow me to explain my perspective: When I engage in prayer for someone, I begin by opening my heart and connecting with the infinite unconditional love that is the essence of my being. From there, I project a beam of love-light energy through time and space, directing it to the heart of the person I am focused on. I offer this love and light as a means of support for their personal growth and highest good, whatever that may entail. I do not attempt to control the outcome; I simply send them supportive energy. How they choose to utilize that energy is entirely up to them.

You have within you the ability to engage in your own version of this type of prayer whenever you feel compelled to. First, express gratitude for the blessings in your life. Give thanks to the wisdom of your inner self for all the physical and physiological functions it performs daily, promoting your health, healing, and overall well-being.

Next, mindfully construct your prayer and visualize it taking the form of a seed. Embrace the hope that what you seek through this prayer genuinely serves the person or situation's highest good and optimal development, benefiting all who may be affected by it. Acknowledge that what you are praying for may not necessarily align with the person or situation's greatest good, and be willing to surrender to whatever that may be without becoming attached to a specific outcome. Leave the final result in the hands of Spirit.

Then, create an empowered energy state by employing breathing techniques that help clear the pathway between yourself and the Divine. It is important to address potential blockages in this channel, as they may hinder the actualization of your prayer. Blockages can manifest as feelings of guilt, shame, fear, self-judgment, negativity, or limiting beliefs. Take notice of any thoughts, emotions, or images that may be obstructing the flow and consciously release and cleanse them, allowing the pathway to become clear.

Now, bring your awareness to your abdomen, your center, known as hara in Japanese, dan t'ien in Chinese, and the solar plexus in Western terminology. Take three long, slow breaths into this area, then exhale fully, releasing any tension or tightness from your body.

Empower the seed with several more breaths, observing it growing brighter and stronger. With the next breath, send the seed down into your center. Send five more breaths into the seed, empowering its successful manifestation by imagining that what you seek is already happening. Notice the feelings that arise from this manifestation, and deepen into those emotions. Express gratitude for the manifestation that is on its way to you or the intended recipient.

When you experience the good feelings vibrating at a high level, send the prayer seed up the open channel with a burst of high-level energy, illuminating each chakra in your body until it reaches the highest chakra—the radiant light of the thousand-petaled lotus—enabling the seed to fully blossom. This activates the cosmic web of oneness, through which prayer can be answered.

Always conclude by expressing gratitude for the blessings in your life.

EXERCISES

◀▶ *Favorite Prayers*

♦ May all beings live in freedom, with peace in our hearts, peace in our minds, and peace in the world, with justice and equity for all. May all beings have adequate food, clothing, shelter, health care, education, and meaningful, gainful employment opportunities.

◆ May we joyfully live together in a wisdom society of sisters and brothers in harmonious relationship with each other and with all of creation—restoring, regenerating, and rejuvenating the Sacred Hoop of Life for Fullest Blossoming and Greatest Good for All. May it be so, and may you and I show up to do our part in bringing it to fruition.

◆ May all who cross my path today feel blessed by my presence.

◆ I place my future in your hands, Great Spirit, and I choose to experience inner peace now, feeling joined, connected, and One with You, who has always been and will be always, and who is here right now.

◆ Infinite Light and Love is what I see. Infinite Light and Love is what I be, quantumly connected to non-local infinite cosmic consciousness and all those who have, who do, and who will cross my path, seeing their light being a love giver to all.

◆ I skillfully set my sails with attention, humility, receptivity, fluidity, adaptability, flexibility, and gratitude, to catch the winds and waves of God's grace with all that crosses my path today, successfully opening the doorway to bring through Fullest Blossoming Greatest Good for All.

◆ I send out healing light and love to all those who have crossed over and all who are crossing over, to those left behind, and all those struggling with illness and pain, all those seeking light through darkness, and all those coming in to bodies, being carried, being born, to all the children, all the elders, and to all those helping in the birthing processes of health, healing, justice, peace, beauty, equity, and freedom.

◀◆▶ *Raise Consciousness Using Songs, Mantras, Chants*

The following phrases can be sung, chanted, repeated to yourself silently, or said out loud to help you focus your attention on thoughtforms that will help you Wake Up, Wise Up, and Live Love Now.

- Live Love Now—it's the only time you've got.
- The sun returns, the sun returns, the sun returns. Honor the darkness, feed your soul, and you will surely grow.
- Live with the Spirit, live with the light, live with love, and you will be all right.
- Peace abides, wisdom guides, love provides.
- Love is the answer. Love is the key. Love is the healer.
- Let love flow through me.
- Let the tower tumble. Let the ego program crumble.
- Open the door. Time to explore. Reap the reward. More and more.

I often recite this gratitude chant, which uses *Ya-wee*, a Coastal Miwok word for "thank you."

> *Ya-wee.*
>
> *Ya-wee.*
>
> *Ya-wee for you and me.*
>
> *Ya-wee. Ya-wee.*
>
> *Ya-wee for you and me.*
>
> *Ya-wee.*
>
> *Ya-wee.*
>
> *May We All Be Free.*
>
> *May All Beings Be Happy.*
>
> *May All Beings Be Safe.*
>
> *May All Beings Everywhere Be Free.*
>
> *It Starts Right at Home with You and Me.*
>
> *Ya-wee.*

WAKING UP AND WISING UP TO LIVE LOVE NOW

All the things I've talked about in this book can be summarized with these key reminders:

- ◀ Sense, feel, listen.
- ◀ Look, see, observe.

◄ Wise Up.

◄ Remember Live the Love that you are Now.

◄ Pull the plug on unconsciously conditioned virtual reality dreams.

◄ Co-create with Spirit a conscious dream.

◄ Weave wisely.

◄ A new vision of living based on Love.

◄ Dissolve sources of pain and suffering originating from ego identity, self-importance, or taking things personally based on illusionary perceptions of separation.

◄ Raise the sparks of your divinity for fullest blossoming and greatest good, serving Higher Will, walking your Heart Path to Completion with Joy, Grace, and Gratitude.

◄ Give thanks.

◄ Live Love Now.

Use the *Starlight Song* to energize your Wake Up, Wise Up, Live Love Now process by singing along with the video of the song at this link audio.innertraditions.com/psychedelicshaman.

STARLIGHT SONG

We are stardust brought to Earth,
we are stardust brought to birth,
we are stardust brought to life
to shine, shine, shine.

Do you know why you are here,
filled with light and love so dear?
Do you know why you are here?
To shine, shine, shine.

Polish up the light you are,
come so far, from a star,
polish up the light you are
to shine, shine, shine.

How to polish a star so bright?
Hold it up into the light.
No more fussing no more fight,
you hold it up to the light.

Shine on into darkness.
Shine on into night.
Shine on when it's cloudy.
Shine with all your might.

It's all about the wisdom
that lives in you and me,
doesn't cost a penny—
it's absolutely free!

When you get its message,
there's no place left for fear.
We are all together,

all together here.

Thank stardust for its message.
Thank stars for sending it through.
A gift from the cosmos,
straight to me and you.

It's a gift to remember.
It's a gift to see the truth.
Stardust is our life force,
it gives you a big boost.

What blocks you from shining?
Is it judgment, guilt, or shame?
Whatever clogs your pipes,
give it a name.

Look it in the eye,
then let it go.
Play a new game,
with stardust as your claim.

Your light is needed
in today's stressful world.
The star that you came from
shines from afar.

Sending you strength
to remember who you are.
Stand and be counted.
Be your own star.

The dust of you is magic.
Let it flow, let it grow.

The stardust you are made of,
just want to know.

Are you ready?
Are you ready?
Are you ready?
Let's Go!

Today is for shining.
It's all up to you.
Today is the day you're given
to bring your light through.

Growing light of love,
growing love of light,
growing light of love,
will help you through the night.

Growing light of love
will help you to see,
deep down inside
the light is in you and me!

Let it shine,
let it shine,
let it shine!

Open your heart and be kind.
Right now
is always the best time.

So let it shine,
let it shine,
let it shine!

CLOSING WORDS

Ruth's Truths

Let us take heart, my friends. We undeniably possess the ability to create a world that works for all its inhabitants—a world that is fair, just, healthy, happy, and peaceful. However, this can only be achieved if a sufficient number of us embrace our role as Psychedelic Shamanic Wisdom Warriors and actively engage in the necessary work. In support of that end, I close by sharing what my mother, Ruth, said to me before her death at the age of ninety-five.

Ruth lay in a semi-comatose state at my sister Briane's home in rural New Hampshire. My sisters Ilsa, Briane, her two daughters, and I sat in a semicircle around her bed. Silently, we watched her struggle to breathe. Each breath came slower and shallower. Then, suddenly, she sat up in bed, looked me straight in the eye, and delivered a message that reverberated in the room with the power of a temple gong rung in a cavernous hall.

Love is the glue that holds us together. Love rules the world.

Then she laid back down and returned to the semi-comatose state. That was it. *No mas.* She died peacefully shortly thereafter.

Flying back home to California, I couldn't help but reflect on the power of my mother's dying message. I think she was spot-on with the first part of what she said: "Love is the glue that holds us together." It is an interesting synchronicity that quantum physicists use the term "gluon" to refer to a particle whose sticky function holds quarks together, thereby enabling the creation of what we experience as the material world.

It is the second part of what she said, "Love rules the world," that I offer to you as a hopeful prediction of the kind of future you and I can help create—one in which love indeed is the operating principle by which we live our interconnected lives.

May it be so.

All Blessings. Love,

Tomás

(aka Dr. Tom Pinkson, Tomika, Poppy, and Popsters)

APPENDIX

Cultural Appropriation

We stole land,
killed,
scalped,
deliberately distributed
smallpox infested blankets,
destroying cultures,
twenty-thousand-year-old people
who loved their children,
honored their elders,
killed by lance of avarice and greed,
minds honoring gold, forsaking soul.
So much lost
people endured,
survived,
making a stand,
listen to
stories and songs, struggling to be heard
from those who remember
how to be.

— tomás —

UNDERSTANDING CULTURAL
(MIS) APPROPRIATION

Those of us socialized by Eurocentric values, myths of white suprem-acy, and settler colonialism need to Wake Up and see the truth of what has been historically done and is still being done to People of Color and Indigenous people around the world. Those of us who feel called to the wisdom ways of Indigenous spirituality and culture, whether from the Americas or any other place in the world, need to learn how to be in respectful relationship with Indigenous people. We must ensure that we are not taking from or exploiting them for our personal gain at their expense, as has been our historical pattern.

Over time, I have learned that right-relationship means that tak-ing without giving back in a meaningful way constitutes cultural theft, appropriation, and a continuation of colonialist exploitation. I have learned that giving back involves developing an ally relationship based on mutual respect and exchange. This entails understanding how the ideology of white supremacy leads to discriminatory and rac-ist policies that are deeply embedded in social, educational, economic, and health institutions, privileging Caucasians and oppressing People of Color.

I needed to learn from Native people about the issues they hold as concerns, the discriminatory, racist, and prejudicial political, edu-cational, health, legal, and economic policies and institutions that actively oppress their lives today. I needed to learn about the causes of the incredible poverty, alcoholism, drug abuse problems, high rates of suicide, and violence to women—much of which stems from decades of forced residential school attendance that destroyed families. I needed to learn about treaty violations with sovereign nations.

And it wasn't enough to merely learn about these issues—I needed to actively engage in addressing them, including supporting demonstra-tions and demonstrators for justice, such as the water protection efforts at Standing Rock.

When appropriate, I needed to assist organizers of ceremonies and gatherings in any way I could. This might involve chopping wood for a ceremony or providing transportation for elders to and from ceremonies, stores, medical appointments, or banks to help with financial matters. Sometimes, it meant providing necessary food, clothing, medical supplies, and, when possible, financial support to the community I was working with at the time.

I needed to create a respectful ally relationship with a balance between giving and taking. This meant listening before speaking, taking the time to learn from my Native mentors about which ritual behaviors and spiritual practices were acceptable for me to participate in or use in my own life and which were not. Throughout this learning journey, I have always found Native people to be open, kind, and generous when they feel respected and cared for as fellow human beings and when they receive support in ways that are meaningful to them.

CALL TO ACTION
Organizations to Support

Native American Rights Fund

The Native American Rights Fund holds governments accountable. We fight to protect Native American rights, resources, and lifeways through litigation, legal advocacy, and legal expertise. Since 1970, the Native American Rights Fund (NARF) has provided legal assistance to Native American tribes, organizations, and individuals nationwide who might otherwise have gone without adequate representation. NARF has successfully asserted and defended the most important rights of Indians and tribes in hundreds of major cases, and has achieved significant results in such critical areas as tribal sovereignty, treaty rights, natural resource protection, voting rights, and Indian education.

With credibility built over fifty years of service, NARF has become a respected consultant to policymakers and others in drafting legislation. As a consensus builder, NARF works with religious, civil rights, and other Native American organizations to shape the laws that will help assure the civil and religious rights of all Native Americans. NARF attorneys, many of whom are tribal citizens, use their understanding of Indian legal issues to assist tribes in negotiating with individuals, companies, and governmental agencies.

Native American Rights Fund
950 F Street, NW, Suite 1050
Washington, DC 20004
(202) 785-4166
narf.org

Cultural Survival

An Indigenous-led NGO and U.S. registered nonprofit that advocates for Indigenous people's rights and supports Indigenous communities' self-determination, cultures, and political resilience worldwide since 1972. We envision a future that respects and honors Indigenous people's inherent rights and dynamic cultures, deeply and richly interwoven in lands, languages, spiritual traditions, and artistic expression rooted in self-determination and self-governance.

The core of our efforts rests on supporting and amplifying efforts and raising awareness for Indigenous communities. Cultural Survival has curated a robust network of partnerships with Indigenous communities spanning over seventy countries on six continents.

Cultural Survival
2067 Massachusetts Avenue Cambridge, MA 02140
Phone: 617-441-5400

Wixárika (Huichol) Research Center

We are committed to the defense of the sacred lands, native culture, and natural resources of the Wixárika people. In addition to our direct work within the Wixárika communities, we maintain an ongoing publicly accessible news section, where we continually upload press reports to keep our readers up to date with the Wixárika people's efforts to recover territory, their ongoing defense of sacred pilgrimage sites, and the challenges they face today in a world that is rapidly changing all around them.

Email: inquiries@wixarika.org

Phone: 510-420-1231

Tribal Trust Foundation

Our mission is to support the preservation of Indigenous cultures and wisdom through philanthropy and education in order to promote living in harmony with nature and each other. Since 1996, the Tribal Trust Foundation has identified sustainable grassroots cultural preservation projects to support Indigenous people worldwide. We partner with local organizations whose experience and existing relationships with specific tribes can sustain joint initiatives over the long term, to help preserve the living arts and traditional wisdom of Indigenous people. Our focus is on capacity building and empowerment processes wherein communities can initiate the holistic change they wish to manifest. Tribal Trust Foundation possesses a unique ability to reach, connect with, and help preserve these Indigenous cultures and people through education, documentation, promotion, donor driven trips, and financial support.

Tribal Trust Foundation

P.O. Box 5687

Santa Barbara, CA 93150

info@tribaltrustfoundation.org

The Earth Charter

The Earth Charter is a document that provides an ethical foundation for actions to build a more just, sustainable, and peaceful global society. Its sixteen principles are powering a global movement; when applied to your business, school, or community, you begin turning conscience in to action to help make all life on Earth thrive.

The Earth Charter articulates a mindset of global interdependence and shared responsibility. It offers a vision of hope and a call to action. Thousands of people and organizations worldwide have been inspired by this vision, and are working independently at local levels while collaborating globally, contributing to the transition to sustainable ways of living on the planet.

Earth Charter International
c/o University for Peace
P.O. Box 138 6100
San José, Costa Rica
Phone: +506 2205-9060
info@earthcharter.org

SUGGESTED READING

ADDITIONAL BOOKS
BY TOM PINKSON

*The Shamanic Wisdom of the Huichol: Medicine Teachings
for Modern Times*
Fruitful Aging: Finding the Gold In The Golden Years
Do They Celebrate Christmas in Heaven?
The Gift of Mantra
Walking a Sacred Road: On Pilgrimage with the Huichol
The Starlight Song Story Book

ADDITIONAL INFORMATION
ABOUT PSYCHEDELICS

How to Change Your Mind by Michael Pollan
Plant Intelligence and the Imaginal Realm by Stephen
Buhner
"LSD and the Anguish of Dying, Neural Correlates of
the Psychedelic State as Determined by fMRI Studies
with Psilocybin" *Harper's Magazine*, September 1965,
by Robin Carhart-Harris, et. al.

THE SCIENCE BEHIND
EXPANDED CONSCIOUSNESS

The Quantum Revelation: A Radical Synthesis of Science and Spirituality by Paul Levy

Quantum Mind: The Edge Between Physics and Psychology by Arnold Mindell

Physics and Philosophy: The Revolution in Modern Science by Werner Heisenberg

Foundations of Physics by Steve Adams

Cosmology of Consciousness: Quantum Physics and the Neuroscience of Mind by Deepak Chopra, Helge Kragh, Michael Mensky, Nicholas Campion, and Roger Penrose

BOOKS ON INDIGENOUS
AND SHAMANIC WAYS

The World We Used to Live In: Remembering the Powers of the Medicine Men by Vine Deloria Jr.

Lame Deer, Seeker of Visions by John (Fire) Lame Deer and Richard Erdoes

Black Elk Speaks by John G. Neihardt

The Inner Journey: Views from Native Traditions edited by Linda Hogan

Blackfoot Physics: A Journey into the Native American Universe by F. David Peat

An Indigenous Peoples' History of the United States by Roxanne Dunbar-Ortiz

Grandmothers of the Light: A Medicine Woman's Sourcebook by Paula Gunn Allen

The Sacred: Ways of Knowledge, Sources of Life by Peggy V. Beck, Anna Lee Walters, and Nia Francisco

Braiding Sweetgrass: Indigenous Wisdom, Scientific Knowledge, and the Teachings of Plants by Robin Wall Kimmerer

WAKING UP BOOKS

Waking Up: Overcoming the Obstacles to Human Potential by Charles T. Tart

Beyond Ego: Transpersonal Dimensions in Psychology edited by Roger N. Walsh and Frances Vaughn

The Art of Being and Becoming by Hazrat Inayat Khan

Merchants of Light: The Consciousness That Is Changing the World by Betty J. Kovács

GLOSSARY

A Course in Miracles (**ACIM**): A spiritual self-study program designed to awaken us to the truth of our oneness with God and Love.

agape love: The highest form of love; contrasted with eros, or erotic love, and philia, or brotherly love.

aikido: A modern Japanese martial art, translated as "the way of unifying (with) life energy" or as "the way of harmonious spirit," whose primary goal is to overcome oneself instead of cultivating violence or aggressiveness.

aloha consciousness: Symbol of the Hawaiian culture and lifestyle: respect and love one another and live in harmony with everything around you.

anima: The feminine part of a man's personality.

Anishinaabe: Group of First Nations people belonging to that particular cultural and linguistic family.

assemblage point: A place in our body's energy field that functions like a camera lens, an opening, an aperture that lets in only what it has been unconsciously conditioned to pay attention to as being "reality" from the socio-cultural world we are born to and that our family was conditioned by. The awareness of a newborn infant is totally open to all bandwidths of energy flowing into it. Gradually, the infant and growing child learns which of those energies to pay attention to and which do not help the child get its needs met. The child's assemblage point begins to close off certain inputs, and after a while the child loses awareness of their existence. The aperture has narrowed. As discussed in the book, there are ways of shifting or reopening the assemblage point back to awareness of a broader range of what the universe is giving us, raising our consciousness of who we are, what we are, why we are here.

Attitudinal Healing: A cognitive approach to healing the judgment, blame, shame, and self-condemnation that blocks awareness of love's presence.

ayahuasca: A plant based psychedelic from the Amazon Basin.

collective unconscious: The part of the unconscious mind that is derived from ancestral memory and experience and is common to all humankind, as distinct from the individual's unconscious.

consciousness: The fact of awareness by the mind of itself and the world.

cosmology: The science of the origin and development of the universe.

Deer Spirit: A totem animal guide in the spirit world.

5-MeO-DMT: A hallucinogenic tryptamine drug that occurs naturally in many plants and animals.

Hopi: Native American tribe that lives primarily on the Hopi Reservation in northeastern Arizona, United States.

humanistic psychology: A perspective that emphasizes looking at the whole person and the uniqueness of each individual.

inner child: The part of your subconscious that was picking up messages way before it was able to fully process what was going on.

Kauyumari: Huichol term for the Blue Deer Spirit.

kensho: Japanese term, from the Zen tradition, for an initial insight or awakening to seeing one's true nature.

Lakota: One of the bands of the Sioux Nation.

"look-within" place: A reference to the process of introspection; going within to find wisdom.

los gringos en el Norte: North Americans.

machismo: Exaggerated focus on masculine behavior, values, and attitudes.

medicina: Substances and healing skills used to open consciousness to higher states than ego for attunement and communion with the spirit realm.

medicine people: Individuals who have gone through intensive initiation training, under the guidance of elders, in learning how to elicit altered states of consciousness to access power from the spirit world to help them in their healing services.

mindfulness: The basic human ability to be fully present, aware of where we are and what we're doing, and not overly reactive or overwhelmed by what's going on around us.

monkey mind: A reference to ego consciousness jumping randomly around from moment to moment.

moon time: A woman's time of menstruation.

nierica: The doorway to transpersonal states of consciousness.

numinous: Having a strong religious or spiritual quality; indicating or suggesting the presence of a divinity.

Oglala Sioux: Also known as the Oglala Lakota Nation, one of the seven bands of the Titowan (Lakota) division of the Great Sioux Nation.

ohana: Hawaiian word for extended family.

patriarchal conditioning: A system of social structures and practices in which men dominate, oppress, and exploit women.

pranayama: An ancient breathing technique that originates in yogic practices from India and involves controlling your breath in different styles and durations.

projecting: Unconsciously taking unwanted emotions or traits you don't like about yourself and attributing them to someone else.

psyche: Your mind and your deepest feelings and attitudes.

psychedelic journey: An altered state induced by taking a psychoactive substance or substances.

psychedelic substance: A loosely grouped class of substances capable of inducing altered thoughts and sensory perceptions.

Qigong: A system of coordinated body postures with movement, breathing, and meditation used for the purposes of health, spirituality, and martial arts training.

quantum field: The basic underlying energy substratum of reality.

right relationship: Respectful interactions of balance and harmony.

shaman: A person who utilizes altered states of consciousness for healing and service to their community.

somatic: Referring to the physical body.

spiritual activist: Someone who works for change in society from a spiritual framework.

spiritual curriculum: The tests of your life.

Starlight Ohana: Humanity, as all of us are made of stardust brought to Earth.

"strengthening the container": Building up the fitness of physical, emotional, mental, and spiritual being.

T'ai Chi: A Chinese discipline involving very slow physical exercises to help your mind relax and improve your body's balance in harmony with the universe.

Takutsi Nakaway: Huichol term for the Goddess Great Grandmother Growth.

tantric: Hindu and Buddhist esoteric traditions, techniques, and rituals primarily focused on the cultivation and buildup of kundalini energy.

Tao: The natural order of the universe, whose character one's intuition must discern to realize the potential for individual wisdom.

Tayaupa or Taupa: Huichol term for Father Sun.

tikkun olam: Hebrew term for healing the wounds of the world.

totem spirit: A kinship or mystical relationship with a spirit-being, such as an animal or plant.

transpersonal higher consciousness: an awareness of aspects of the human experience that transcend the sense of a separate self.

trickster: An entity that fools you by its tricks, busts and humbles ego hubris, and teaches you about deeper reality.

tuki: Huichol term for a special structure holding ceremonial items.

Turtle Island: Indigenous term for North America.

Two Leggeds: Human beings.

unconscious macho habituation: Being stuck in a machismo way of living that stems from conditioned beliefs and values deep in the psyche.

Wakan Tanka: Sioux term that translates as "Sacred Mystery."

ACKNOWLEDGMENTS

This book is the result of a team effort.

At the onset of this project, I brought the raw material to Shams Zairys, who provided excellent first draft editing.

The next pass went to Mary Bernstein, who continued with the "massaging" of my sprawling text into a cohesive form.

Final editing went to my daughter Kimberly Pinkson, who went through every word and skillfully shapeshifted the material to a meaningful flow that helped better communicate this book's ideas.

And to round out the team was Roger Clay, who brought his supportive, creative skills and insights to manifesting the finished product's layout and imagery, helping me put the final polish on its content.

In the background of all my work is Andrea, Kimberly, and Nicole, my wife and daughters who support me through the trials and tribulations I put them through in the labor process of birthing a book. Eternal gratitude!

Great Gratitude to all the labor coaches, for without them, the material would have remained an undelivered mishmash. Hopefully our efforts will prove meaningful to readers who seek to reconnect with their sacred selves and the divinity of the cosmos.

THANK YOU.

—TOMÁS

ABOUT THE AUTHOR

 Tom Soloway Pinkson, Ph.D., aka tomás, is a transpersonal psychologist and medicine man of the spirit. He serves as a guide, counselor, mentor, and vision quest and ceremonial leader, and is the author of many books, including *Shamanic Wisdom of the Huichol: Medicine Teachings for Modern Times*. His life has been devoted to inspiring people to awaken and live from the truth of their infinite light and love.

Tom's work is based on more than sixty years of studying and blending Western psychology, shamanism, contemporary and ancient wellness practices, neuroscience, and the latest findings from quantum physics. He serves as a bridge builder, translating Indigenous wisdom into a modern context. Tom has worked with wisdom elders in various locations around the world, including the Amazon jungle, the Andes Mountains, Hawaii, the Yukon, Ireland, Hungary, Bali, and North, Central, and South America. Notably, he completed an eleven-year apprenticeship with Huichol shamans in Mexico.

Tom was an early leader in integrating vision quests, rite of passage work, and positive psychology to American health and wellness practices. He also contributed to the field of psychedelics for healing and spiritual growth. Additionally, he played a role in establishing the first at-home hospice program in the United States. Tom is the founder of the nonprofit foundation A New Vision of Living as well as the New

Vision of Living online course and Live Love Now Group, which meets monthly. Both offerings provide spiritual medicine teachings and practices for a new vision of living based on love. Furthermore, Tom developed the "Shamanic Wisdom for Fruitful Aging" course for the Shift Network.

Most recently he developed a live performance piece, the *Traveling Cosmic Magic Mojo Medicine Show*, using song, music, story, and ceremony to share the fruits of his life's work.

Currently residing in California, Tom lives with Andrea, his wisdom-woman wife of over fifty years.

INVITATION FROM THE AUTHOR

You can access more support for growing Psychedelic Shamanic Wisdom Warrior consciousness through my Live Love Now Group, a live cyberspace community. Learn more about the group at drtompinkson.com/livelovenow and by listening in on my weekly "Shamanic Sundays" offerings on Facebook and Zoom. I am also available for individual sessions for spiritual counseling and psychedelic integration work.

I would love to hear from you, and welcome any feedback, comments, or questions about my work and this book. Email me directly at tompinkson@gmail.com.

If you found this book meaningful, please let your friends and networks know about it. I also always appreciate a positive review on Amazon or Goodreads. Thank you for helping to spread the good word.